Rita Cheminais' Handbook for New SENCOs

Leading and Coordinating SEN Provision

Rita Cheminais

SAGE

Los Angeles | London | New Delhi
Singapore | Washington DC

First published 2010

SAGE Publications Ltd
1 Oliver's Yard
55 City Road
London EC1Y 1SP

SAGE Publications Inc.
2455 Teller Road
Thousand Oaks, California 91320

SAGE Publications India Pvt Ltd
B 1/I 1 Mohan Cooperative Industrial Area
Mathura Road
New Delhi 110 044

SAGE Publications Asia-Pacific Pte Ltd
33 Pekin Street #02-01
Far East Square
Singapore 048763

Library of Congress Control Number: 2010922900

British Library Cataloguing in Publication data

A catalogue record for this book is available from the
British Library

ISBN 978-1-84920-095-0
ISBN 978-1-84920-096-7 (pbk)

Typeset by C&M Digitals (P) Ltd, Chennai, India
Printed by CPI Antony Rowe, Chippenham, Wiltshire
Printed on paper from sustainable resources

Rita Cheminais' Handbook for New SENCOs

I would like to dedicate this book to all those newly appointed SENCOs working towards achieving the National Award for Special Educational Needs Coordination, who have found this resource invaluable in enabling them to get to grips with the SENCO role, and in helping them to increase the participation and achievement of pupils with SEN and/or disabilities in the education settings in which they are working.

Contents

About the author

Rita Cheminais is a leading expert in the fields of special educational needs (SEN), inclusion and Every Child Matters in maintained primary, secondary and special schools, and in local authority children's services.

With a background as a teacher, an SEN Coordinator, an OFSTED inspector, a General, Senior and Principal Adviser in SEN and Inclusion, and as a School Improvement Partner, Rita has 33 years of practical experience.

She is a prolific writer and respected author of journal articles and books in the areas of SEN, inclusion and Every Child Matters. Rita speaks regularly at national conferences and was one of the three 'Ask the Experts' participating in the Becta National Grid for Learning (NGfL) live online national inclusion conference in 2003. Rita provided consultancy on inclusion for the Rolls-Royce Science Prize national initiative for schools in 2004. During May to September 2009, Rita was commissioned by the DCSF to undertake research on National Indicator 50: the Emotional Health of Children. Her publication entitled *Effective Multi-Agency Partnerships: Putting Every Child Matters into Practice* was shortlisted for the NASEN Book to Promote Professional Development Award 2009.

Currently, Rita is an independent freelance education consultant with Every Child Matters (ECM) Solutions. She provides keynote presentations at conferences, as well as offering support and consultancy to educational settings wishing to achieve the Every Child Matters Standards Award and/or the Multi-Agency Partnership Award.

Every Child Mattters (ECM) Solutions:
email: admin@ecm-solutions.org.uk
website: www.ecm-solutions.org.uk

Acknowledgements

Thanks are due to Jude Bowen, Senior Commissioning Editor at Sage Publications, for encouraging me to write this essential book in response to the government's national SENCO training programme.

I wish to acknowledge the valuable feedback I have received from the many SENCOs I have been privileged to meet during my travels as a keynote speaker at conferences across the country. They have helped to inform the contents of this book.

I also wish to thank the DCSF, OFSTED, QCDA, RAISE online, the Audit Commission and the TDA for giving me permission to make reference to some of their materials relating to SEN and disability, the SENCO role and the national SENCO training framework. Thanks are also due to Moira Thompson, Headteacher of Hawthorns Community School, for giving permission to use Figure 1.2.

Special thanks go as usual to Philip Eastwood, SENCO and AST at St Mary's and St Paul's C of E Primary School in Knowsley, for keeping me in touch with the realities of being a SENCO in the twenty-first century. I also wish to thank all those colleagues from higher education institutions, local authorities, NASEN and educational publishing who continue to promote and refer to my work.

I am also indebted to Amy Jarrold, Assistant Editor at Sage Publications, and all those who have helped to make this book a reality.

Introduction

This book provides the essential definitive handbook and training manual for the national SENCO training programme, covering all the TDA specified learning outcomes. It should be used and read in conjunction with key SEN official government publications.

The book is not only appropriate for all those newly appointed SENCOs working in early years settings, maintained primary and secondary schools, academies and short stay schools, but also for existing SENCOs, who wish to update their current knowledge on aspects such as financial planning and budget management for SEN, using and analysing data, deploying staff and managing resources.

The book will also be relevant to all those training providers from schools, local authorities, higher education institutions and independent training organisations who will be delivering the approved national SENCO training across the country. Each chapter focuses in depth on one of the five TDA key learning outcomes specific to the SENCO training framework, which cover:

- the professional context

- the strategic development of SEN policy and procedures

- the coordination of provision

- leading, developing and supporting colleagues

- working in partnership with pupils, families and other professionals.

The role of the special educational needs coordinator (SENCO), as we know it today, has taken 16 years to evolve, as illustrated by the timeline in Chapter 1 (Table 1.1).

In a nutshell, the role of the SENCO in the twenty-first century, as outlined in the SEN Coordinator Regulations (HMSO, 2008), includes:

- informing a parent that their child has special educational needs

- identifying the pupil's special educational needs

- putting in place and coordinating the additional provision for SEN children

- monitoring the effectiveness of SEN provision

- maintaining and updating SEN pupil records

Opportunities	Challenges/dilemmas
• Enhanced status through membership of the senior leadership team • Building the capacity of the school's workforce to identify SEN and remove barriers to learning and participation • Strategic manager of resources – financial (SEN budget) and human • Strategic planning – provision mapping • Quality assurer – value for money, evaluating impact of additional provision on SEN pupils' outcomes • Champion and advocate for SEN children and their parents/carers • Manager of change and problem-solver – data analysis, action research on what works well for SEN pupils • Manager of partnerships with the wider children's workforce • Team builder – managing and maintaining professional relationships between a range of stakeholders	• Expanding role as Every Child Matters systems embed, e.g. CAF, TAC, Lead professional, extended services • Reducing time spent working directly with SEN pupils • Balancing the ever-increasing number of government initiatives and strategies that assume SENCO involvement • Maintaining a healthy work-life balance while continuing to be overburdened by the paperwork of bureaucratic systems such as the CAF and the SEN Code of Practice

- liaising with and keeping parents/carers of SEN pupils informed about their child's SEN and additional provision

- ensuring relevant information about the child's SEN and SEN provision is passed on to the next education setting

- promoting the inclusion of SEN children in order to ensure access to the school's curriculum, facilities and extra-curricular activities

- recruiting, training and supervising teaching assistants who work with SEN children

- advising other teaching colleagues on differentiated teaching methods and personalised learning approaches for individual SEN pupils

- contributing to in-service training for staff at the school on SEN

- preparing and reviewing SEN policy and provision.

The SENCO in the twenty-first century faces a number of new opportunities and some interesting challenges and dilemmas, pertaining to their strategic role. These can best be summarised in the table opposite.

The book is unique and groundbreaking in bringing together in one concise volume all the essential and important information and good practice required of newly appointed SENCOs to enable them to meet the requirements of the National Award for SEN Coordination. The resource includes downloadable materials which can be tailored and customised accordingly. It also includes useful points to remember and further activities at the end of each chapter.

To all those SENCOs using this resource, I do hope you find it invaluable in enabling you to ensure SEN pupils receive the high-quality educational provision that enables them to make progress in their learning and well-being.

How to use this book

The nationally approved training programme for newly appointed SENCOs is very broad, and covers many topic areas. There is an expectation that a SENCO will be able to complete the course part-time in one year. This may pose a challenge to those newly appointed SENCOs starting in the role completely from scratch. However, this book may go some way towards enabling new SENCOs to meet such a challenge by offering a comprehensive handbook and training manual which covers each of the five TDA learning outcomes in sufficient depth, to support the successful completion of the national training programme within a tight timescale.

This resource will enable new SENCOs to understand:

- the statutory and regulatory frameworks and developments in SEN

- the high incidence of SEN and disability, their effect on pupil participation and learning, and strategies for improving SEN pupil outcomes

- the strategic development of SEN policy and procedures, including financial planning, budget management and best value principles

- how to coordinate provision and deploy and manage staff and resources effectively

- how to collect, analyse and use SEN pupil-level data

- how to lead, develop and provide professional direction to the work of other staff in school in relation to SEN

- how to work in partnership with pupils, families and other professionals

- how to engage, consult and communicate with pupils, parents/carers and other colleagues.

The book can be worked through systematically in chapter order, or it can be dipped into, focusing on particular topics and aspects.

Each chapter provides a summary of what will be covered; key information; checklists offering practical tips; examples of good practice; photocopiable and downloadable resources which can be customised and adapted to suit the type of education setting; useful points to remember; further activities for assignments, reflection and professional development, as well as signposting to further resources and information.

Overall, the book provides an essential resource that can be used:

- to act as a point of reference for busy SENCOs, including SENCO training providers

- to inform a more consistent approach in SENCO national training

- to enable pages to be photocopied for developmental purposes within the purchasing institution

- to promote further discussion and encourage reflection on SEN policy, provision and the SENCO role

- to support the national modules of training for SENCOs who are new to the role.

Downloadable Materials

This book is supported by a wealth of resources that can be downloaded from www.sagepub.co.uk/ritacheminais for use in your setting. A full list of the resources available is below:

Chapter 1

Chapter 2

Chapter 3

Chapter 4

Chapter 5

Key for icons

 This chapter covers

 Points to remember

 Further activities

 Downloadable materials

 Photocopiables

List of Figures and Tables

Figures

Tables

1

The professional context of SEN

> **This chapter covers the following TDA SENCO learning outcomes:**
>
> - **the laws and guidance on SEN and disability equality**
> - **data protection and confidentiality, health and safety**
> - **the principles and outcomes of Every Child Matters (ECM)**
> - **how schools can help pupils with SEN and/or disabilities to achieve the ECM outcomes**
> - **the contribution of extended services in improving outcomes for pupils with SEN and/or disabilities.**

The laws and guidance on special educational needs (SEN) and disability

Newly appointed SENCOs will need to familiarise themselves with the SEN and disability equality legislation and guidance. The timeline in Table 1.1 signposts SENCOs to the relevant legislation and key guidance documents, many of which can be downloaded from the following websites:

http://publications.dcsf.gov.uk/

www.teachernet.gov.uk/sen/

www.dcsf.gov.uk/everychildmatters/

The Disability Equality Duty

The Disability Equality Duty (the Duty) applies to all schools requiring them to take a more proactive approach to promoting disability equality and eliminating discrimination. The Duty, which was introduced into the Disability Discrimination Act 1995 (DDA) in 2005, specifies:

- a general duty to promote disability equality

- a specific duty to prepare and publish a disability equality scheme.

Table 1.1   SEN, disability and ECM timeline 1981–2010

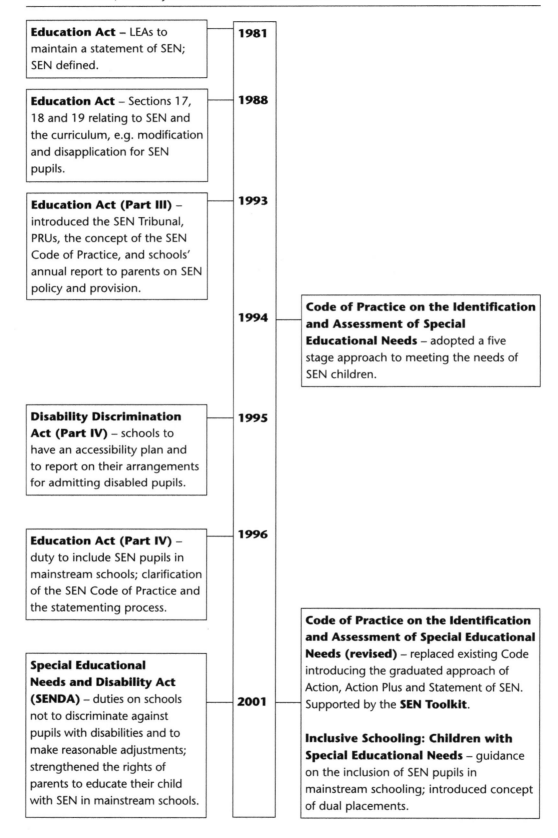

Education Act – LEAs to maintain a statement of SEN; SEN defined.

1981

Education Act – Sections 17, 18 and 19 relating to SEN and the curriculum, e.g. modification and disapplication for SEN pupils.

1988

Education Act (Part III) – introduced the SEN Tribunal, PRUs, the concept of the SEN Code of Practice, and schools' annual report to parents on SEN policy and provision.

1993

1994

Code of Practice on the Identification and Assessment of Special Educational Needs – adopted a five stage approach to meeting the needs of SEN children.

Disability Discrimination Act (Part IV) – schools to have an accessibility plan and to report on their arrangements for admitting disabled pupils.

1995

Education Act (Part IV) – duty to include SEN pupils in mainstream schools; clarification of the SEN Code of Practice and the statementing process.

1996

Code of Practice on the Identification and Assessment of Special Educational Needs (revised) – replaced existing Code introducing the graduated approach of Action, Action Plus and Statement of SEN. Supported by the **SEN Toolkit**.

Special Educational Needs and Disability Act (SENDA) – duties on schools not to discriminate against pupils with disabilities and to make reasonable adjustments; strengthened the rights of parents to educate their child with SEN in mainstream schools.

2001

Inclusive Schooling: Children with Special Educational Needs – guidance on the inclusion of SEN pupils in mainstream schooling; introduced concept of dual placements.

Table 1.1 *(Continued)*

	2002	**Access to Education for children and young people with medical needs** – statutory guidance on the education of children unable to attend school due to medical needs. **Accessible Schools: planning to increase access to schools for disabled pupils** – guidance on increasing curriculum and physical access to schools, and access to information. **Special Educational Needs: a mainstream issue** – report of the Audit Commission on SEN children's education and provision.
	2003	**The Report of the Special Schools Working Group** – acknowledged the continuing role of special schools in supporting mainstream inclusion. **Every Child Matters** (Green Paper) – outlining the government's vision and proposals for improving services for children and young people, and specifying five ECM well-being outcomes for all children.
The Children Act – provided legislative framework for ECM by improving vulnerable children's well-being outcomes, including those with SEN and/or disabilities; introduced ECM systems: CAF, lead professional, ContactPoint, NSF, safeguarding, integrated inspection of children's services; introduced Children's Centres, and expanded the extended school programme.	**2004**	**Every Child Matters: Next Steps** – set out the timetable for implementing the Children Act 2004. **Every Child Matters: Change for Children in Schools** – outlined expected changes and introduced the ECM Outcomes Framework. **Removing Barriers to Achievement: The Government's Strategy for SEN** sets out the improvements required in SEN policy, practice and provision, focusing on four aspects: early intervention; removing barriers to learning; raising expectations and achievement; and delivering improvements in partnership.

(Continued)

Table 1.1   *(Continued)*

Disability Discrimination Act (DDA) – built on earlier legislation of 1995 by bringing in the Disability Equality Duty (DED) (general and specific duties), and requirement of schools to prepare and publish a disability equality scheme, and strengthened parents' right to appeal to SENDIST if the school failed to comply with the DED.	**2005**	**Managing Medicines in Schools and Early Years Settings** – replaced previous guidance of 1996, and provided advice on developing a Policy for Medicines, the safe administration of medicines, and drawing up Health Care Plans. **Special Educational Needs: A New Look** – Mary Warnock's policy document requested a radical review of SEN, the SEN Framework and Inclusion Framework.
Education and Inspections Act – clarified the role of the SENCO, requiring them to be a qualified teacher; ensured fair access to schools for pupils, irrespective of their ability, social background, ethnicity and disability; governing bodies to promote pupils' ECM well-being.	**2006**	**House of Commons Education and Skills Committee's Report on Special Educational Needs** (July) – identified the problems existing in the government's SEN and inclusion processes and made a number of recommendations relating to improved SEN CPD for teachers, with the SENCO being a member of the senior management team in schools. **Government's Response to the Education and Skills Committee Report on Special Educational Needs** (October) – requested OFSTED to undertake a review of the SEN Framework 2009–2010, and proposed an Inclusion Development Programme (IDP) focused on high-incidence SEN.
	2007	**Implementing the Disability Discrimination Act in Schools and Early Years Settings** – government guidance on putting the DDA into practice, with exemplification of including disabled children in schools and early years settings. **Aiming High for Disabled Children (AHDC): Better Support for Families** – the government's transformation programme for disabled children's services focused on three priorities: access and empowerment; responsive services and timely support; and improving quality and capacity, e.g. providing short breaks.
Special Educational Needs (Information) Act – required information about SEN children in England to be published annually in order to inform future action and improvements at LA and	**2008**	**Inclusion Development Programme (IDP)** – interactive web-based CPD SEN resource for all teachers launched, with the first materials focusing on dyslexia and speech, language and communication needs from early years through to primary and secondary phases of education.

Table 1.1 *(Continued)*

	2009	
school levels, in SEN pupils' ECM well-being outcomes. **The Education (Special Educational Needs Co-ordinators) (England) Regulations** – the SENCO to be a qualified teacher and the governing body to monitor the effectiveness of the SENCO. Clarified and specified the role of the SENCO.		IDP is a four-year programme, which continues to roll out between 2009 and 2011, covering high-incidence SEN: autism, BESD and MLD. **The Bercow Report: A Review of Services for Children and Young People (0–19) with Speech, Language and Communication (SLC) Needs** – 40 resulting recommendations to improve services for children and young people with SLCN. Prompted government to fund research into SLC good practice and enhancing augmentive communication.
The Education (Special Educational Needs Co-ordinators) (England) (Amendment) Regulations – requires governing bodies to ensure the new SENCO undertakes nationally approved training to obtain the National Award for Special Educational Needs Coordination.		**Lamb Inquiry – Special Educational Needs and Parental Confidence** – review focused on improving parental confidence in the SEN assessment process, improving information for parents of SEN children and improving outcomes for children with SEN. **Identifying and Teaching Children and Young People with Dyslexia and Literacy Difficulties (Rose Report)** – 19 recommendations related to assessing and advancing children's progress; improving school support; and strengthening intervention programmes by establishing one-to-one tuition for dyslexic pupils. **Progression Guidance 2009–2010** – aimed at raising expectations about the progress of SEN pupils, based on their age and prior attainment. Provided data sets in the NC core subjects as well as P Scale point-score equivalents. **Children with Special Educational Needs 2009: An Analysis** – first DCSF annual SEN statistical publication in response to the SEN Information Act 2008. It focused on data relating to types of SEN; attainment and progression; Absences and Exclusions; and the views of SEN pupils (from the TellUs Survey).

The Duty is necessary in view of schools:

- providing education to pupils, some of whom may have a disability

- being an employer where some employees may have a disability

- being a universal service provider to pupils, parents and community members, some of whom may be disabled.

The Disability Equality Duty also requires schools to have due regard for the need to:

- promote equality of opportunity between disabled people and other people

- eliminate discrimination that is unlawful under the DDA

- eliminate disability-related harassment

- promote positive attitudes towards disabled people

- encourage the participation of disabled people in public life

- take steps to meet disabled people's needs, even if this requires more favourable treatment

- monitor staff and pupils by disability.

The Duty reinforces the DDA, by ensuring schools:

- increase the extent to which disabled pupils can participate in the school curriculum

- improve the school environment to increase the extent to which disabled pupils can take advantage of education and associated services

- improve the delivery of information to disabled pupils, to the standard which is provided in writing for pupils who are not disabled.

SENCOs will find the DfES (2007c) resource, *Implementing the Disability Discrimination Act in Schools and Early Years Settings*, invaluable in supporting the implementation of the DDA within their setting.

Developing a Disability Equality Scheme (DES)

All schools, academies, city technology colleges and city colleges for technology of the arts are obliged to produce a DES. This scheme shows how the setting is going to meet the general and specific disability equality duty. The DES can be a stand-alone equality policy or it can be embedded within another strategic document such as the school development plan. In either case, the DES must be closely linked with the school's Accessibility Plan, which in turn informs the school's disability action plan. The DES had to be implemented by 3 December 2007 in schools, and must be revised every three years.

What schools must set out in their DES

A school's DES must specify:

- the way in which disabled people, i.e. pupils, staff and parents, have been involved in its preparation

- the arrangements for gathering information and evidence on the effects of its policies on:

  - the recruitment, development and retention of disabled employers

  - the educational opportunities available to, and the achievements of, disabled pupils.

- the methods for assessing the impact of its existing or proposed policies and practices on disability equality

- the steps it will take to meet the general duty, as outlined in the its disability action plan

- the arrangements for putting the information gathered into use, i.e. in relation to informing the review of the effectiveness of its disability action plan and preparing subsequent DESs.

Factors to consider when developing and revising a DES

- A senior manager should take the lead on the DES. This may be a deputy head teacher, assistant head teacher or the SENCO.

- The governor(s) with responsibility for equality, inclusion and SEN need to be engaged in the development and review of the DES with the senior manager.

- The views of disabled pupils, parents and staff must be gathered to inform the DES and its review.

- Evidence from Section A of the school's OFSTED self-evaluation form (SEF) should inform the DES and its review.

- Financial resources and premises planning information needs to inform the DES and its update.

- Advice and guidance from the local authority will be valuable in supporting the school on the development and review of its DES.

- The review of the DES needs to judge what has been its impact and the developments that still need addressing.

The school's accessibility plan can be extended and strengthened to meet the requirements of the disability equality scheme.

Freedom of information

SENCOs need to be aware of the Freedom of Information Act 2000, which came into force on 1 January 2005. This Act deals with access to official information, and was introduced to promote greater openness and accountability. This Act made it a legal right for any person to ask a school for access to the information it holds. The Freedom of Information Act 2000 recognises the need to protect sensitive information in certain instances. Schools are under a duty to provide advice and assistance to anyone requesting information.

An enquirer of information is entitled to be told whether the school holds the information they want, except where certain exemptions apply. There is a need to preserve confidentiality and protect sensitive material in some circumstances, for example in relation to individual children. The SENCO cannot withhold information in response to a valid request unless one of the following applies:

- there is an exemption to disclosure

- the information sought is not held

- the request is considered to be vexatious or repeated

- the cost of compliance exceeds the threshold of £500.

Any requests for information should be dealt with within 20 days, excluding school holidays. It is an offence to damage, destroy or conceal information in response to answering such an enquiry. A valid freedom of information request should always be made in writing (which can include facsimile or email), and it should state the name of the enquirer and their address and also give a description of the information they require. An enquirer does not have to state why they require the information. Any expressions of dissatisfaction regarding the request for the information by an enquirer will be dealt with through the school's existing complaints procedure.

It is the responsibility of the governing body to ensure a school complies with the Freedom of Information Act. If a SENCO is asked for any information about SEN provision or about any SEN pupils by someone external to the school, such as a local councillor, they must inform the head teacher and the governing body immediately, and not pass on any information unless the governing body has approved the request.

It is important to follow the school's policy and procedures in relation to information sharing, data protection and confidentiality. The school should have a 'publication scheme' in place which sets out the information they already hold that is publicly available.

The SENCO must keep a record of all requests made for SEN information, and log any refusals and the reasons for not providing the required SEN information. Information can be provided if it has already been made public.

Data protection

The Data Protection Act 1998 requires all schools and other organisations who handle personal information to comply with eight data protection principles which state that data must be:

- fairly and lawfully processed

- processed for limited purposes

- adequate, relevant and not excessive

- accurate and up to date

- kept no longer than necessary (e.g. finance data should be kept for six years, and staff and pupil data for seven years)

- processed in accordance and in line with data subjects' rights

- secure

- not transferred to other countries without adequate protection.

The SENCO will need to be familiar with the school's 'acceptable use policy' in relation to checking on electronic information technology usage and access. Information sharing is a key area of data protection compliance and one in which SENCOs will be engaged, particularly where a CAF is undertaken and when the SENCO may also be designated as the 'Lead Professional' for a SEN pupil and involved in the 'team around the child' process.

The following list of questions will help SENCOs to comply with the Data Protection Act and to follow the appropriate procedures when sharing information with other professionals and agencies:

- Do I really need this information about an individual SEN pupil?

- Do I know what I am going to use the information for?

- Do those whose information I hold know that I've got it, and are they likely to understand what it will be used for?

- If I am asked to pass on personal information, would the adults/pupils about whom I hold information expect me to do this?

- Am I satisfied the information is being held securely, whether it is on paper or held electronically?

- Is the website or intranet I use secure for information sharing?

- Is access to personal information limited to those with a strict need to know?

- Am I sure the personal information is accurate and up to date?

- Do I delete or destroy personal information as soon as I have no more need for it?

- Have I trained my learning support staff in their duties and responsibilities under the Data Protection Act, and are they putting them into practice?

Under the Data Protection Act 1998, certain information is exempt from disclosure which can be shared with other professionals as service providers. This includes:

- material where its disclosure would be likely to cause serious harm to the physical or mental health or emotional condition of the pupil or someone else

- information about whether the child is, or has been subjected to, or may be at risk of, suspected child abuse

- references about pupils supplied to potential employers, student admissions bodies, another school, a higher education/further education institution or any other place of education or training

- information that may form part of a court report.

SENCOs will need to familiarise themselves with the school's policy relating to pupils' safe use of the internet, school website, educational chat rooms, email, blogs, mobile telephones and other portable information technology such as Personal Digital Assistants (PDAs) in lessons.

Confidentiality

Information is confidential if it is sensitive, not already in the public domain or given to you in the expectation that it will not be shared with others. Confidential information can be shared if you have the consent of the person who provided the information or the person to whom the information relates. Confidential information can be shared without consent if there is an over-whelming 'public interest', e.g. to prevent significant harm occurring to a child or to others; to prevent a serious crime happening; or when you have been ordered to do so by a court of law. A young person is able to give consent in their own right, for information about them to be shared, irrespective of age, as long as they have sufficient understanding about what sharing information means.

The school or other setting a SENCO works in should have a 'need to know' policy in operation relating to confidentiality and information sharing. Such a policy makes the following explicit:

- what information is required

- under what circumstances the information can be released

- to whom it is appropriate to release the information

- how the information will be used

- how the released information will be crucial to improving outcomes for the child or young person concerned

- when written consent is required for the release of information.

Any confidential conversations that take place among professionals about an SEN child must take place in a private sound-proofed office. All staff should be made aware of ContactPoint and what its purpose is and how it is to be used. (This will be covered in the last chapter of the book.)

Protocols for confidentiality and information sharing

The appropriate sharing of information is crucial to ensuring that vulnerable pupils, which includes those with SEN, get the services and support they require in order to secure positive learning and well-being outcomes. The DCSF provides seven golden rules for information sharing which can be found in their publication *Information Sharing: Pocket Guide (2008g)*. In summary, these rules cover the following:

1. **Recognise that the Data Protection Act is not a barrier to sharing information.**

2. **Be open and honest** with the child/young person and/or their family as to why, what, how and with whom information will or could be shared.

3. **Seek advice** if in any doubt, without disclosing the identity of the child or young person concerned.

4. **Share information with consent where appropriate.** The SENCO may still share information without consent if, in their professional judgement, the lack of consent can be overridden in the public interest.

5. Base information sharing decisions on considerations of the **safety and well-being of the child** concerned and others who may be affected by the actions.

6. Ensure that the information shared is **necessary** for the purpose for which you are sharing it; that it is only shared with those people who need to have it; that it is **accurate** and up to date; and that it is shared **securely** in a **timely** fashion.

7. **Keep a record** of what information has been shared, with whom and for what purpose.

What to do if a pupil makes a disclosure to the SENCO

A newly appointed SENCO should use the following guidance when a pupil makes a disclosure in their presence.

1. Reassure the pupil that they are right to tell you and that they are not to blame for what has happened to them.

2. Don't promise the pupil not to tell anyone else but explain to them that you have to make certain that they feel safe, and therefore you may need to ask other adults to help you ensure this happens.

3. Listen to the pupil carefully and do not question them. Ask the pupil to tell you what they want to tell you and no more.

4. When the pupil has finished making the disclosure, make sure they feel safe and explain what you are going to do next.

5. Write down notes on what the pupil has told you while it is fresh in your mind. The notes should include the following information: the date, time and place where the disclosure was made. They should also include the names of all adults present when the pupil made the disclosure. The record of the pupil's account should use their exact words. The SENCO must sign the notes and then pass them on to the school's child protection officer or, if that person is the SENCO, pass it on to the head teacher immediately.

6 The SENCO must ensure they receive feedback on the outcomes of their referral, and also get a professional debriefing, if the pupil's disclosure has been particularly traumatic to listen to.

Health and safety legislation

Schools have to comply with the duties set out in the Health and Safety at Work Act 1974, and the subsequent Management of Health and Safety at Work Regulations 1999, which cover risk assessment.

Under the Health and Safety at Work Act, the governing body of a school is required to ensure the health and safety of their staff and pupils (a duty of care). SENCOs must follow the procedures and protocols as outlined in the school's health and safety policy.

Health and safety legislation links closely with the Disability Discrimination Act, which requires the governing body and head teacher of a school to consider whether they have taken 'reasonable steps' by amending their health and safety policies, procedures and practices to ensure pupils with SEN and/or disabilities are not placed at a substantial disadvantage.

The SENCO needs to ensure that health and safety legislation does not deny pupils with SEN and/or disabilities access to educational opportunities, or compromise their dignity. Further information about health and safety legislation is available from the Health and Safety Executive website (www.hse.gov.uk).

Risk assessment and pupils with SEN and/or disabilities

Inclusion and advances in medical science have brought more pupils with physical disabilities and medical needs into mainstream schools, who may require specialist handling, special aids and facilities, specialist therapies, minor medical treatment on school premises or the administration of medication during the school day. The SENCO needs to work in partnership with a range of health professionals such as the school nurse, physiotherapists and occupational therapists, as well as with the parents/carers of the pupil, in order to ensure that they have up-to-date information and knowledge on what it is reasonable to expect and deal with on the school premises, and outside school, on any residential, educational or sporting trips or events.

A risk assessment is simply a careful examination of what could cause harm to a pupil(s) or staff to enable the person in charge – in this case, the SENCO – to weigh up whether they have taken enough precautions and if they need to do more to prevent potential harm occurring. It is a dynamic, ongoing, sustainable process that is a legal requirement in terms of recording and keeping under review. The purpose of a risk assessment is to balance health and safety considerations with the prevention of unreasonable restrictions on a pupil with SEN and/or disabilities and their right to equality of opportunity, dignity and privacy.

A risk is defined as the chance, whether high or low, of someone being harmed, together with an indication of how serious that harm could be.

Risk assessments are undertaken at the early planning stage of any educational in-school or out-of-school activity or event, and also in advance of a pupil with SEN and/or disabilities being admitted to a school, college or work placement, which may pose potential health and safety risks. An alternative activity (Plan B) must always be prepared and risk assessed, in the event of the pupil not being able to participate in the main activity with their peers on the day.

SENCOs will be familiar with the five steps to undertaking a risk assessment, which are:

1. Identify the hazards (a hazard is anything that may cause harm).

2. Decide who might be harmed and how.

3. Evaluate the risks and decide on any precautions.

4. Record the findings and implement them.

5. Review the assessment and update if necessary.

The SENCO must ensure that the risk assessment shows that:

• a proper check has been made

• they have consulted with those who might be affected

• they have dealt with all the significant hazards, taking into account the number of staff/pupils/people who could be involved

• the precautions are reasonable and the remaining risk is low

• relevant staff, the pupil and the child's parents or carers have been involved in the process.

The SENCO will allocate in-class support to those pupils with physical or sensory impairments, or more complex medical needs in practical subjects such as Design and Technology, Science and PE, and ask the teacher to check these pupils wear protective clothing and work at benches of an appropriate height, if they are wheelchair users.

SENCOs will find the DfES (2003e) CD resource, *Success for All: An Inclusive Approach to PE and School Sport,* an invaluable resource.

SENCOs need to ensure that they, and their team of teaching assistants/learning support assistants, are familiar with the relevant health and safety regulations relating to: manual handling; the use of display screen equipment; exposure to hazardous substances; infection control; and the administration of medicines, for which there should be a school medicines policy in place. The Health and Safety Executive website (www.hse.gov.uk) provides access to the above-mentioned regulations.

An example of a risk assessment template is illustrated in Table 1.2.

Procedures for the administration of medicines to pupils

All pupils with medical needs will have a healthcare plan in place, which identifies the necessary health and safety measures required to ensure that they and/or their peers are not put at risk. This will also give details about any medication that the child or young person takes before or during the school day, indicating the resulting side effects, which may cause barriers to learning for the pupil, e.g. tiredness, poor concentration or memory.

There is no legal duty on school staff to administer medicines. The requirement to do so should be indicated in the job descriptions of relevant staff. Any staff who administer medication to pupils in school need to have been appropriately trained by health professionals.

SENCOs will find clear guidance on the administration of medication to pupils within the DH/DfES (2005) document *Managing Medicines in Schools and Early Years Settings*.

The principles and outcomes of Every Child Matters

Every Child Matters (ECM) was first proposed by the government in September 2003, in response to the tragic death of Victoria Climbie. The timeline in Table 1.1 lists the legislation and key reports pertaining to the development and implementation of ECM.

The concept of Every Child Matters

The concept of Every Child Matters is to protect, nurture and improve the life chances and well-being of all children and young people from birth to age 19 and, in particular, those who are vulnerable, disadvantaged and most at risk of abuse and neglect, which does include pupils with SEN and/or disabilities, and those in public care.

We know that children and young people cannot learn effectively if they feel unsafe, or if health problems create barriers to their learning. For this reason, ECM adopts a holistic approach, focusing on the needs of the whole child or young person, that is, their learning and well-being needs as defined by the five Every Child Matters outcomes:

- **Be healthy** – enjoying good physical, sexual and mental health and having a healthy lifestyle.

- **Stay safe** – being protected from harm, abuse, neglect, bullying and discrimination.

Table 1.2 Template for a risk assessment

School name:		Date of risk assessment:	
Activity venue:		Date of activity:	
Brief description of the nature of the activity:			
List of actual hazards	Who is affected	Risk rating (Low, Moderate or High)	
Key areas where potential hazards may occur	Control measures (action being taken)		
Group/pupils involved:			
Staffing details:			
Equipment:			
Venue/environment:			
Travel arrangements:			
Emergency procedures:			
RISK ASSESSMENT REVIEW			
Date of risk assessment review:			
Any significant changes affecting the risk assessment:			
Nature of the revision required to the risk assessment:			

- **Enjoy and achieve** – enjoying attending school and recreation; behaving well, achieving optimum potential.

- **Make a positive contribution** – being involved in volunteering and with the community; being involved in decision making; not engaging in anti-social behaviour.

- **Achieve economic well-being** – being prepared and ready for life after school and the world of work; acquiring basic skills in literacy and numeracy ICT.

ECM aims to reduce inequalities and levels of educational failure, ill health, substance misuse, teenage pregnancy, crime, anti-social behaviour, abuse, neglect and child poverty. Schools are not expected to tackle these issues alone, but to work in partnership with other agencies and organisations.

The governing body of maintained schools, under Section 38(1) of the Education and Inspections Act 2006, has a duty to promote the well-being of pupils at a school. They also have to regard the local authority's Children and Young People's Plan, and any views expressed by parents of registered pupils.

The Principles of Every Child Matters

Ten principles underpin Every Child Matters. These are as follows:

1. All children and young people are to fulfil and reach their optimum potential.

2. Early intervention and prevention through improved service provision is crucial.

3. Safeguarding and protecting children and young people from harm, neglect and poverty is of paramount importance.

4. A well-trained, skilled, knowledgeable and flexible children's workforce is essential.

5. Improving information sharing between agencies is key.

6. Better coordinated, joined-up, integrated front-line services are vital.

7. Greater accountability through an increased focus on the impact of provision on outcomes for children and young people is necessary.

8. Children and young people have a right to voice their views and inform decision making in relation to personalised services and learning.

9. Communities need to be made safer and provide recreational and voluntary activities for children and young people to participate in.

10. Improving access to advice, information and services for parents/carers and families on positive parenting, family learning, childcare, adoption and fostering is crucial.

The ECM Change for Children programme has created many challenges for schools and SENCOs. These include:

- a greater focus on impact and outcomes, rather than on processes and systems

- a greater commitment to enhancing parents'/carers' and pupils' rights and empowerment

- increased partnership working with a wider range of external practitioners

- understanding the different roles and responsibilities of the members of the wider children's workforce

- understanding new procedures and systems, e.g. the Common Assessment Framework (CAF), the National Service Framework (NSF), the ContactPoint and information sharing protocols, Team Around the Child (TAC) and the Lead Professional role.

The implications of these changes brought in by ECM are illustrated in Figure 1.1.

How pupils with SEN and/or disabilities can achieve the ECM outcomes

The latest OFSTED inspection framework clearly indicates the expectations as to what all pupils, including those with SEN and/or disabilities, can achieve in relation to the five Every Child Matters (ECM) well-being outcomes. SENCOs should refer to the inspection judgement grade descriptors (OFSTED, 2009: 15–18, 21–4, 26–7).

In addition, the SENCO will need to take into account the school-level indicators for pupil well-being, when evaluating and reviewing the progress of pupils with SEN and/or disabilities. For example:

- What has the pupil's attendance rate been like over the year?

- Which SEN pupils have been persistent absentees?

- Which SEN pupils have been excluded from school (fixed term and permanent exclusions)?

- How many SEN pupils have a school lunch and how healthy is it?

- How many SEN pupils undertake at least two hours of PE/sport each week?

- Which extended school activities are these pupils accessing and what has been the impact of these on their learning and well-being?

- (Secondary sector only) How many SEN pupils on leaving school go on to further training, education or employment?

SENCOs need to identify in which of the five ECM outcomes pupils with SEN and/or disabilities achieve the best. They also need to identify the ECM outcomes in which these pupils make the least progress, why that may be the case, and what action can be taken to address any of the gaps existing in these well-being outcomes.

In addition to collecting quantitative evidence of SEN pupils' progress in the ECM outcomes, SENCOs will also wish to gather directly qualitative evidence on ECM, via pupil voice and surveys. Both quantitative and qualitative ECM evidence findings can be incorporated into pupils' annual statement reviews. Figure 1.2 gives an example of an ECM statement review cover sheet, which a SENCO may wish to utilise. Figure 1.3 provides a model survey for gathering pupils' views about their ECM outcomes, which can be customised.

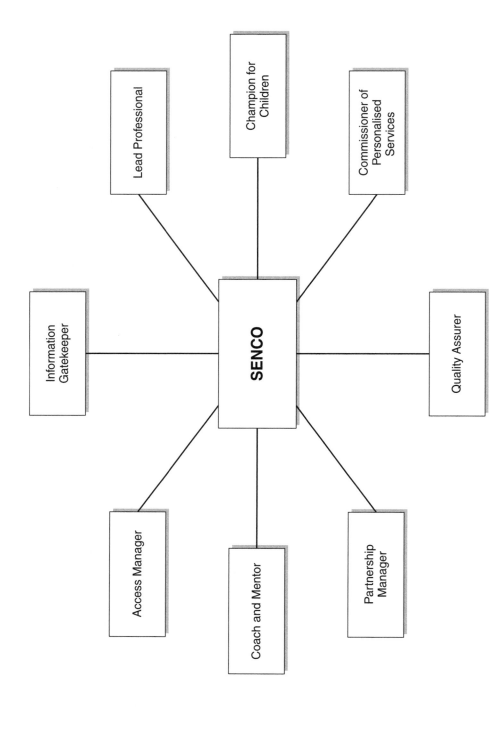

Figure 1.1 ECM and the implications for the SENCO role

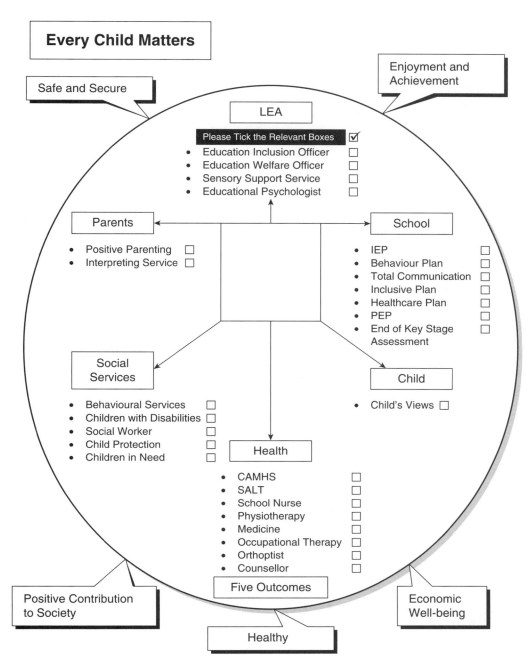

Figure 1.2 ECM cover sheet for an annual statement review
Reproduced with kind permission of Hawthorns School

Photocopiable:
Rita Cheminais' Handbook for New SENCOs © Rita Cheminais, 2010 (SAGE)

1. How safe do you feel in school?

2. How well does the school sort out bullying?

3. Who would you go to in school to talk to, if something is worrying you?

4. How has the school helped you to be healthy and lead a healthy lifestyle?

5. How are you helped to learn and make good progress at school?

6. If you need extra help or support with school work, who provides this?

7. Is pupil behaviour in school good, bad or OK?

8. Are you and other pupils treated fairly and with respect by staff in school?

9. How well do school staff listen to your views and those of other pupils, to make things better for pupils?

10. How does the school help you to understand and respect pupils from different cultures?

11. Are you and other pupils able to think of ideas and ways of helping others?

12. How does the school help pupils to manage their own feelings and behaviour?

13. Does the school offer a good range of lunchtime and after-school clubs and activities for pupils?

14. How does the school help you and other pupils to get life skills for the future?

15. What is good about being a pupil at your school?

Figure 1.3   Pupil survey on the ECM outcomes

Photocopiable:
Rita Cheminais' Handbook for New SENCOs © Rita Cheminais, 2010 (SAGE)

This ECM information can also be fed into the school's self-evaluation form, and reported back to governors annually. Table 1.3 maps how schools are enabling pupils with SEN and/or disabilities to achieve the five ECM outcomes.

The contribution of extended services in improving SEN pupil outcomes

Extended services delivered through schools and children's centres and other community settings make significant contributions to meeting the ECM outcomes.

The aim of an extended school and children's centre is to work in partnership with other agencies and with the local community, acting as a service hub, to meet local needs. Having a range of health, social care and education practitioners based on or near the site of a school is beneficial when developing a coordinated approach to removing pupil barriers to learning and participation. The government defines an extended school as one that provides a range of services and activities beyond the school day and is open 8 a.m. to 6 p.m. This core offer comprises of:

- **high quality wrap-around childcare** available all year round from 8 a.m. to 6 p.m.

- **a varied menu of activities** on offer, to include provision such as a breakfast club, homework club, study support group, sports activities, music tuition, dance, drama, arts, crafts and special interest clubs, volunteering activities, business and enterprise activities, visits to museums and art galleries

- **parenting support** including information sessions for parents at phase transfer, information about national and local sources of advice, guidance and information, parenting programmes run with the support of external partners and family learning sessions

- **swift and easy referral** to a wide range of specialist support services such as speech therapy, child and adolescent mental health services (CAMHS), family support services, intensive behaviour support for young people and sexual health services

- **wider community access** to ICT, sports and arts facilities, including adult learning opportunities.

Extended services may be delivered not only by individual schools but also in partnership with local public, private or voluntary community sector providers, via a cluster or federation of schools, or through co-location with a children's centre. It is important that the SENCO knows which extended services pupils with SEN and/ or disabilities are accessing, and to know the impact in contributing to improving their learning and well-being outcomes.

OFSTED (2006b, 2008b) and the DCSF (Walllace et al., 2009) have found that children and young people who access extended services have:

- increased self-esteem, motivation, aspirations and positive attitudes to learning and school

- improved attendance at school

Table 1.3 How SEN pupils can achieve the five ECM outcomes

Be healthy	Stay safe	Enjoy and achieve	Make a positive contribution	Achieve economic well-being
Circle time sessions	Access to CAMHS support	Transfer and transition activity programme cross-phase/key stage	School Council	Mini-enterprise activities
Access to a trained counsellor	Key adult system	Positive rewards system for pupils	Youth Parliament	Pupil Takeover Day
Social stories	Peer buddy system – playground pals	High-quality ICT provision for pupils	ECO group and recycling	Work experience
Learning mentor support	Restorative justice	Booster and catch-up sessions	Peer mentoring and buddy system	School bank
PSHE activities (drug, alcohol and sex education)	PSHE – stranger danger, road safety	Homework club	Community projects/ volunteering opportunities	Family fun days and social events
Healthy school meals	Cycling proficiency award	Good range of lunchtime and after-school clubs	SEAL	Key skills
Five fruits or vegetables a day	Internet and mobile technology safety sessions	Adult mentor for every pupil	Hear by Right	Study support – exam techniques
Access to drinking water	Robust child protection procedures in place	Summer school activities	Charity and fund-raising activities	Motivational learning programme
PE and sport activities during and after school	Effective anti-bullying and behaviour policy and procedures	Family learning activities	Annual international/ multi-cultural week	Computer club – preparing a CV
Walking bus	Risk assessments	Behaviour and attendance support programme and tracking system	Annual summer fair	
Cookery club	Pupil ID cards (smart cards/swipe cards) to access school buildings	ECM and curriculum activity weeks	School magazine	
School nurse drop-in sessions	Traffic calming outside school	Artists/poets in residence		
Breakfast club				
Relaxation and massage				
Health Promotion Week				

- improved attainment levels

- improved behaviour

- improved personal and social development.

SENCOs may find the NCSL/TDA (2009) resource useful.

> **Points to remember**
> - Not all pupils with disabilities have SEN.
> - SEN and disability is everyone's responsibility in the education setting.
> - Pupil well-being, inclusion and raising standards go hand-in-hand.
> - Extended school activities help to improve SEN pupils' outcomes.
> - Change is an ongoing developmental process.
> - Following data protection and information-sharing protocols is crucial.

 Further activities

The following questions, focused on aspects covered in this chapter, meet the requirements of the National Award for Special Educational Needs Coordination, and support reflection and professional development:

1. How far do you agree or disagree that the government's SEN Framework needs reviewing, in light of Every Child Matters?

2. To what extent are risk assessment and health and safety legislation limiting some extra-curricular/out-of-school activities and opportunities for pupils with SEN and/or disabilities?

3. What impact are extended services having on pupils with SEN and disability in your school/setting?

4. Which aspect of SEN and disability presents the greatest challenge to you in your role as a SENCO, and how can you address this issue?

5. Some staff in school think that SEN and inclusion conflicts with the standards agenda. Describe how you will convince them otherwise.

Downloadable materials

For downloadable material for this chapter visit www.sagepub.co.uk/ritacheminais

Figure 1.2 ECM cover sheet for an annual statement review

Figure 1.3 Pupil survey an the ECM outcomes

Table 1.2 Template for a risk assessment

2

The strategic development of SEN policy and procedures

> **This chapter covers the following TDA SENCO learning outcomes:**
>
> - the strategic leadership of SEN policy and practice
> - working strategically with senior colleagues and the SEN governor
> - reporting on the effectiveness and impact of SEN policy and provision
> - strategic financial planning, budget management and best value principles
> - provision mapping
> - making effective use of ICT to manage SEN systems
> - strategies for improving outcomes for pupils with SEN and/or disabilities.

The strategic leadership of SEN policy and practice

Strategic leadership entails anticipating change or events, envisioning possibilities, maintaining flexibility, and empowering others to create strategic change as necessary. This type of leadership involves managing through others by adopting a team approach to gain consensus and solve problems.

A SENCO's power of persuasion and influence to inspire others towards achieving common goals and shared values relating to SEN, is driven by their vision for SEN and their passion to do the very best for pupils with special educational needs within a school.

A SENCO, as an effective strategic leader, will not be afraid to make difficult yet pragmatic decisions, particularly when they relate to the best use of resources, i.e. the effective deployment of teaching assistants. Working in a multi-agency environment helps to broaden a SENCO's experience, perspectives and expertise as a strategic leader of SEN. This enables them to think creatively and to seek new ways of working, e.g. by utilising distributed leadership to develop others professionally and build capacity.

An increased emphasis on the strategic role of SENCOs in the twenty-first-century school has resulted in the expectation that they will be respected members of a senior leadership team, thereby demonstrating the importance attached to SEN by head teachers and governing bodies.

The key aim of being strategic is knowing what a SENCO wants to achieve in relation to SEN across a whole school, justifying the direction of travel taken and finding the best ways to get there in order to reach their ultimate goal. This approach influences SEN policy; it also informs the SEN strategy, and the priorities on the SEN development plan, and the SEN priorities on the school improvement plan. Figure 2.1 provides a model template for a SEN development plan, which a SENCO can download and customise accordingly.

There are five key components to effective strategic leadership. These are:

1. Determining a school's strategic direction for SEN – what SEN will look like in the school in three, five and ten years' time.

2. Effectively managing a school's SEN resources (financial and human) – utilising best value principles, which demonstrates good value-added progress, in relation to SEN pupils' outcomes.

3. Sustaining an effective inclusive school culture that welcomes SEN pupils and their parents/carers.

4. Emphasising ethical practice – the moral purpose in 'every child matters', which includes pupils with SEN and/or disabilities, and following each respective code of practice.

5. Establishing balanced organisational controls – i.e. striking a healthy balance between the management of SEN provision and the creative use of the SEN funding available.

Figure 2.2 illustrates the SEN strategic leadership and management process.

Accepting the demands of strategic leadership involves SENCOs making the transition from a familiar operational middle-manager role to the more challenging senior strategic leadership role. SENCOs as strategic leaders must challenge complacency and relentlessly pursue the continual drive for further improvement in relation to SEN pupil outcomes.

With the support of the head teacher, a SENCO in the strategic leadership role will be able to:

• convince staff, governors, parents and carers that SEN pupils' smaller stepped progress is valued within the school

• emphasise that SEN is a collective responsibility, and therefore it is 'everybody's business' within the school

• work in partnership with other agencies within and beyond the school, to meet the needs of SEN pupils

• engage SEN pupils and their parents/carers in informing SEN provision.

Priority 1:

Success criteria:

(i)

(ii)

(iii)

Overall lead person:

Activity	Lead person(s)	Timescale (Start and end date)	Resources (Cost in time and £)	Monitoring (Who, when and how)
1a				
1b				
1c				
1d				
Total resources required:		**Time:** Cost (£):		
Evaluation				

Figure 2.1   SEN development plan template

 Photocopiable:
Rita Cheminais' Handbook for New SENCOs © Rita Cheminais, 2010 (SAGE)

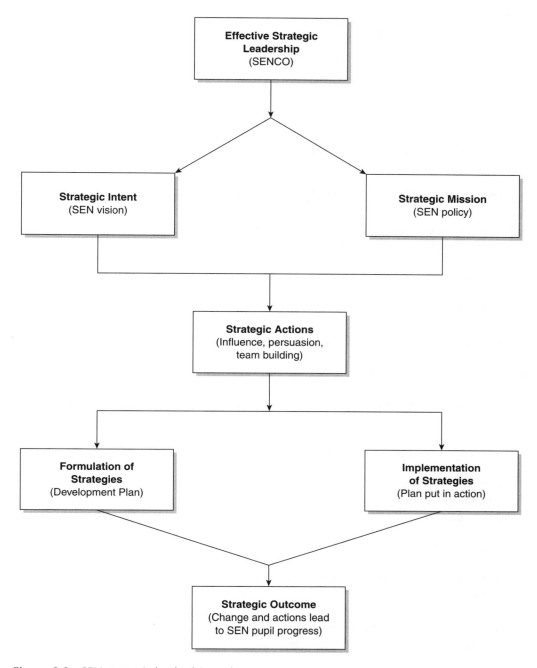

Figure 2.2   SEN strategic leadership and management process

SENCO self-assessment for strategic leadership

In becoming a strategic leader, a SENCO will find it useful to undertake a self-assessment of their leadership skills, in order to identify any strengths and areas requiring further professional development. The following questions can support SENCO self-reflection:

- What are my strengths in leadership?

- How can I capitalise on these strengths?

- What are my weaknesses in relation to strategic leadership?

- What can I do to address these weaknesses?

- Where do I want to be in five years' time?

- How can I get there?

- Do I really want to commit to development?

Building a portfolio of professional development

SENCOs may also value using the following checklist which suggests what to include in a portfolio of professional development.

✓ Job description

✓ Curriculum vitae

✓ Qualification and CRB certificates

✓ Performance management evidence

✓ Certificates of attendance, record of courses attended with evaluations of their impact

✓ Cameos of examples of significant successful SENCO achievements

✓ Relevant extracts from the most recent OFSTED inspection report or other testimonials from the LA, the school improvement partner, parents and carers or SEN pupils

✓ Multi-media evidence, e.g. CD/DVD, photographs, school website

✓ Examples of involvement in successful projects, initiatives and action research on SEN

✓ Evidence of external achievements in SEN, e.g. publications, conference presentations, inputs at local SENCO networks

Managing change

The process of change is developmental, and its purpose is to improve practice and introduce new policies and functions, in addition to altering the 'status quo'. Change brings challenge by working in new ways, especially in changing the attitudes of other colleagues to be more accepting of SEN and disability in view of the opportunities both bring to the school community. Change entails the process of reassessing existing assumptions, beliefs, values and theories relating to SEN and disability. Successful change is dependent on keeping a clear focus on the ultimate goal of improved outcomes for pupils with SEN and/or disability. There are a number of change management models available. One model that SENCOs have found useful is Michael Fullan's (1999) model of change, which is comprised of five dimensions:

1. **Moral purpose** underpinned by values and vision for SEN, with the understanding that the change will make a positive difference.

2. **Understanding change** by encouraging others to 'buy into' the change and capacity building for that change to occur.

3. **Relationship building** which entails developing emotional intelligence.

4. **Knowledge creation and sharing** to raise awareness, develop skills, create and share new knowledge, and think about the strategies for effecting change.

5. **Coherence making** to avoid initiative overload and foster creativity.

SENCOs may find the force field analysis (Lewin, 1943) approach helpful, whereby factors that are likely to support change and prevent the implementation of change are discussed and the strategies for enabling the change to occur are identified.

The strategic leadership of SEN policy

SEN policy in the twenty-first-century school is grounded in school improvement and school effectiveness. The SEN Code of Practice (DfES, 2001b) Regulation 3(1) Schedule 1 provides a detailed framework for a mainstream school SEN policy. The Report of the Lamb Inquiry Review of SEN and Disability Information (DCSF, 2009j) recommended a minimum core of information that should be included in a school's SEN policy. This encompassed:

- information about the school's policies for the identification and assessment of and provision for all pupils with special educational needs

- information about outcomes for children with special educational needs

- how parents can complain about the school's SEN policy or practice

- information about the local authority's SEN policy and where that is published

- information about parents' statutory rights.

  (See DCSF 2009j: 12, para 52.)

Brian Lamb went on to add in the same report that the school SEN policy should be reviewed every three years and revised as necessary, and that parents should be consulted on that policy. He considered that the school's SEN policy should be made widely available, and published on the local authority's website. Brian Lamb also recommended that schools should publish a version of their SEN policy as a leaflet for parents, which should also be widely available. Figure 2.3 provides an example of a model SEN leaflet for a parent.

A Parents Guide to Special Educational Needs at Leafy Lane School

The School SEN Policy

At Leafy Lane School we aim to:

- Meet the needs of the whole child
- Remove barriers to learning
- Raise pupil self-esteem
- Build pupil confidence
- Develop pupil independence
- Provide access to a relevant tailored curriculum

The school SEN policy is reviewed every three years and revised in discussion with parents/carers, pupils, staff and governors.

You can get a copy of the school SEN Policy from the school office or from the school website: www. leafylane.sch.uk

The Local Authority SEN Policy
You can get a copy of the local authority SEN policy from the council website www.anywherecc.gov.uk or ask the SENCO for a copy.

For further information contact the:

SENCO: Rita Gold
SEN Governor: Stan Long
At:
Leafy Lane School
Phone: 09627 118634
Email: rgold@leafylane.sch.uk

Other sources of information and help:

Parent Partnership Service
Offers free impartial advice in confidence.
Phone: 09627 333555
Email: pps.anywhere.org.uk

Publications
Special Educational Needs (SEN) – A guide for parents and carers. Revised 2009

Special Educational Needs Code of Practice

Both are available from: www.direct.gov.uk

Figure 2.3 A model SEN leaflet for a parent

Photocopiable:
Rita Cheminais' Handbook for New SENCOs © Rita Cheminais, 2010 (SAGE)

(Continued)

All about Special Educational Needs

Approximately one in five children will have special educational needs (SEN) at some time during their school career.

This means they may have difficulty with:
- Reading, writing, mathematics
- Understanding information and others and expressing themselves
- Organising themselves
- Sensory perception or physical mobility
- Managing their behavior
- Making friends or relating to adults

These difficulties cause barriers to the child's learning. The school will assess your child to identify their strengths, needs and the extra help they require.

They may be at one of three stages on the SEN Code of Practice, according to need:

Action: extra help in-class from a teaching assistant, small group support, ICT access.

Action Plus: Advice from outside specialists, e.g. specialist teacher, speech and language therapist, health professional.

Statement of SEN: when needs are complex and severe.

What is offered to your child

The school offers the following according to your child's special educational needs:

- Quality first teaching
- A curriculum to match needs
- Enhanced access to ICT or specialist equipment
- In-class support from teaching assistants
- Catch-up programmes in literacy and numeracy
- One-to-one or small group work with a Learning Mentor
- Homework support
- Pupil counseling
- Access to a 'key worker'
- Test and exam concessions
- Extra help from other services

Outcomes for pupils

The extra help the school offers will enable the child to:
- Reach their full potential
- Achieve their personal best
- Make progress
- Feel valued and included
- Enjoy school

Partnership with parents

The school works in partnership with parents to meet the child's needs. This means:
- We listen to the views of parents
- Parents are equal partners in decisions about their child's education
- Parents are kept informed about their child's needs and progress

What parents want to know

- What the school thinks your child's special needs are
- What the school is doing to meet your child's needs
- Whether what the school is doing is working
- How your child feels about what the school is doing to help them
- How parents can be involved

What to do if you have any concerns

- Speak to the teacher and SENCO
- Speak to the SEN Governor and the head teacher
- Get advice from the local Parent Partnership Service

And if your concern is not resolved:
- Follow the school's complaints procedure

Working strategically with senior colleagues and the SEN governor

The governing body of a school has statutory responsibilities for pupils with SEN. The role of the governing body in relation to SEN is outlined in the SEN Code of Practice (DfES, 2001b: 11, para. 1.21).

Most governing bodies of schools will appoint an SEN governor who will have a specific oversight of the school's arrangements and provision for monitoring special educational needs. The SEN governor acts as a critical friend and champion for SEN pupils, working in partnership with the head teacher, the SENCO and the other governors, to ensure SEN remains a core part of a school's decision making. The DfES (2003b) publication, *Making a Difference: A Guide for SEN Governors,* provides a valuable resource for the SENCO to use with a newly appointed SEN governor. In practice, the SEN governor should:

- be clear about the role of the SENCO

- keep up to date with SEN legislation and developments

- attend any relevant SEN governor training locally and nationally

- meet with the SENCO at least once each term to discuss formally SEN issues, policy, provision and ongoing developments

- know how many pupils are on the school's SEN register at any stage and the types of special educational needs within the school

- meet with the learning support team at least once a term to gain insight about their work first-hand, and to view the facilities and resources in use

- listen to the views of SEN pupils about their additional provision

- know the views of parents/carers of SEN pupils in relation to SEN policy and provision within the school

- know the strengths and weaknesses of SEN in the school

- monitor the school's SEN budget to ensure value for money

- have an oversight of the school's SEN provision map

- be kept informed about the progress of SEN pupils

- be kept informed about the views of the school improvement partner about SEN within the school

- seek opportunities to be involved in any local authority SEN working groups or forums

- be involved in the appointment of the SENCO.

Telling questions for the SEN governor to ask the SENCO

1. What is SEN pupils' attendance like and are any of them persistent absentees, or taking holidays in term time?

2. What impact are extended services and additional interventions delivered by multi-agency professionals having on SEN pupils' outcomes?

3. How does the progress made by SEN pupils compare with that of similar schools?

4. How many parental complaints or appeals have been made?

5. How effective has the Parent Partnership Service been in working with the parents/carers of SEN pupils?

6. What has been the impact of any training or INSET attended by or delivered by the SENCO?

7. How are any gaps identified in the school's SEN provision being addressed?

A valuable joint activity for the SENCO to undertake with the SEN governor is to work through the OFSTED criteria for judging the effectiveness of governance, from the perspective of the leadership and governance of the SEN whole school.

Reporting on the effectiveness and impact of SEN policy and provision

Figure 2.4 provides a framework for SENCOs to utilise when they are reporting to the governing body and head teacher on SEN policy and provision.

Strategic financial planning, budget management and best value principles

The SEN funding a mainstream school receives is intended to:

*   support the raising of standards and achievement of SEN pupils

*   support early intervention

*   support the inclusion of SEN pupils

*   safeguard the rights and entitlements of pupils with a statement, and of those with more complex and severe needs to ensure appropriate provision is available

*   demonstrate value for money following best value principles.

Report to the Governing Body on SEN Policy and Provision

SENCO: _____   Date: _____

1. SEN Register update

Key Stage	Action	Action Plus	Statement	Total
EYFS				
Key Stage 1				
Key Stage 2				
			Grand Total =	

Number of pupils moving down a stage on the SEN register _____
Number of pupils coming off the SEN register _____
Number of pupils awaiting a statutory assessment _____

Comments:

2. Effectiveness and impact of additional SEN provision on pupils' outcomes

(Please refer to the attached SEN pupil performance data for the year)

Percentage of SEN pupils making two or more levels of progress across Key Stage 2 in:

English _____   Mathematics _____   in both English and Mathematics _____

Comments:

3. Attendance, exclusions and behaviour of SEN pupils

Percentage of persistent absentees _____   Percentage with 100% attendance _____
Percentage of fixed-term exclusions _____   Percentage of permanent exclusions _____
Percentage of behaviour referrals to BEST team _____

Comments:

4. The effectiveness and impact of multi-agency interventions and support

Comments:

5. The effectiveness of partnership working with SEN pupils' parents/carers

Percentage of parental complaints relating to SEN _____
Percentage of parents satisfied with SEN _____
Percentage of parents attending _____ not attending _____ their child's annual review

Comments:

6. Impact of staff/SENCO SEN INSET on improving SEN pupils' outcomes

Comments:

7. Income and expenditure on SEN
(Please refer to the attached SEN budget breakdown)

Comments:

8. Impact of any SEN developments, projects or initiatives

Comments:

9. SEN governor comments on the strengths and weaknesses in SEN policy and provision existing within the school

Figure 2.4   Template for reporting on SEN to the governing body

Photocopiable:
Rita Cheminais' Handbook for New SENCOs © Rita Cheminais, 2010 (SAGE)

Best value principles

The best value principles comprise of the four 'C's:

Challenge – why, how and by whom an additional SEN intervention is being provided.

Compare – performance outcomes of SEN pupils in relation to the extra provision put in place, with that of similar schools.

Consult – with key stakeholders, e.g. service users, parents/carers to seek their views about the additional provision they have received, and to identify future provision.

Compete – fairly to secure efficient and effective services/additional provision for SEN pupils.

SENCOs are advised to have a regard for the four best value principles when they are planning, provision mapping and procuring SEN resources to meet the needs of SEN pupils.

The Audit Commission's *SEN Value for Money Resource Pack for Schools*

SENCOs, along with school leaders and a school's business or finance manager, will find the online interactive Audit Commission's (2008) *SEN/AEN Value for Money Resource Pack for Schools* invaluable in enabling them to make best use of the available resources for SEN.

The Audit Commission resource pack provides a robust voluntary improvement tool, that takes the school through a seven-stage value for money model for evaluating the impact and outcomes of additional provision on SEN pupils' progress. It enables the school to meet external accountability requirements with the local authority and OFSTED, as well as contributing to the Financial Management Standards in Schools (FMSiS) process.

The resource pack is comprised of a series of self-evaluation audits that each has a bank of statements requiring a response of 'Yes', 'To some extent', or 'No'. The self-evaluation themes cover the following aspects: 1A Income for SEN; 1B Needs identification; 2A Spend on SEN; 2B Provision; 3A Variance (the difference between the total and actual SEN spend and the total and actual SEN income budget); and 3B Outcomes in relation to SEN pupil progress.

SENCOs are likely to find three of the self-evaluation audits the most useful. These relate to Needs, Provision and Outcomes. However, having an overview of the entire Audit Commission Value for Money resource will enable SENCOs to have a greater in-depth knowledge about a school's SEN budget. Examples of the type of statements in the audits of particular relevance to SENCOs include:

Outcomes (3B) Statement 1: *The school actively monitors and reviews the impact of all additional and different provision on individual pupils' experience, progress and outcomes.*

Statement 11: *The school draws routinely on evidence-based research to guide its decision making about which interventions to include in its provision for SEN.*

Statement 14: *All SEN provision made by the school is evaluated and reviewed systematically as part of overall school self-evaluation.*

Once a school's self-evaluation is complete, the statement responses are submitted online and an action plan is generated to support continuous improvement in relation to value for money in SEN provision. The Audit Commission *SEN/AEN Value for Money Resource Pack for Schools* can be accessed at: www.sen-aen.audit-commission.gov.uk

The DCSF and the National Strategies' expectations of SENCOs in relation to their role in respect of the SEN budget are clear, and these are as follows:

- resources are allocated with maximum efficiency, against explicit criteria, published in the school's SEN policy and the school development plan, and against an audit of SEN pupil needs

- there are well-established systems for monitoring and evaluating the impact of additional resources/provision on SEN pupils' progress

- the governors, head teacher, SLT and the SENCO must collaborate over the budget-setting process and management of resources for SEN

- the data relating to the needs of individual and groups of SEN pupils must inform the SEN budget-setting process

- the appropriate governors and senior managers must be able to identify value for money in SEN by relating budget headings to data relating to SEN pupil progress.

Delegation of SEN resources by the local authority

On average, SEN expenditure per pupil equals £1400. A local authority may distribute funding according to the following basic SEN funding formula:

- 10% distributed using social deprivation factors (comprising of 6.6% FSM pupils and 3.4% of pupils living in the most deprived super-output areas)

- 60% distributed on the number of pupils underachieving over the last three years

- 30% allocated according to the number of pupils on the school's SEN register.

A SENCO should ask a school's business or financial manager for a breakdown of the SEN budget at the beginning and end of each financial year.

Table 2.1 provides a useful template for SENCOs to keep a record of SEN income and expenditure over a financial year.

Table 2.1 SEN budget summary template

SEN INCOME – Financial year April 20____ to April 20____		
Income source	**Amount (£)**	**Comments**
Notional school budget for SEN	£	
(includes: delegated amount for statements, action plus and action;	£	
SENCO release time; and % AWPU)	£	
Amount from centrally held LA budget for high cost statements for complex and severe needs	£	
Other funding sources e.g. Dedicated Schools Grant spent on SEN, and any sponsorship funding	£	
	£	
TOTAL SEN Income	£	

SEN EXPENDITURE – Financial year April 20___ to April 20 ___		
Provision	**Amount (£)**	**Comments**
Staffing expenditure (SENCO release time)	£	
Dedicated SEN teaching time (from SEN teachers and SENCO)	£	
Mainstream staff taking smaller, lower-ability sets	£	
Support for SEN from teaching assistants (in-class support and programme delivery)	£	
Administration for SEN Code of Practice, CAF, TAC	£	
Other: (please specify)	£	
External services e.g. outreach; consultancy	£	
Specialist equipment and specialist aids	£	
Curriculum materials and SEN resources e.g. special reading books	£	
Computer SEN software programs	£	
INSET expenditure e.g. supply cover, course fees, travel, trainer fees	£	
Other e.g. enrichment activities, additional midday supervision	£	
	£	
TOTAL SEN Expenditure	£	

 Photocopiable:
Rita Cheminais' Handbook for New SENCOs © Rita Cheminais, 2010 (SAGE)

Provision mapping

A provision map is a strategic management tool, which provides a comprehensive overview and summary of the range of all the additional and different (Wave 2 and Wave 3) provision made available to pupils with SEN/AEN in a school. It also records who is delivering the additional intervention, how frequently this, happens over how long a timescale and at what cost.

The process of provision mapping enhances a school's ability to manage different funding streams more coherently, in order to target particular patterns of additional needs for individual or cohorts of SEN pupils, as well as to plan for the deployment of SEN staffing and build the capacity of staff to meet the needs of SEN pupils. The provision map also enables a SENCO to demonstrate to the governing body, parents/carers, OFSTED, the school improvement partner and the local authority how the SEN budget is being used in order to improve SEN pupils' progress and outcomes. A robust provision management and mapping process, accompanied by an assessment for learning and assessing pupil progress to monitor and track pupil progress, as well as SMART target-setting procedures, will reduce the need to write a whole volume of individual education plans.

Organisation of the provision map

Provision maps can be organised to fit any of the following formats:

- by a particular class or form group

- by year group or Key Stage

- by the five Every Child Matters outcomes

- by whole-school additional needs – the full ability range, including gifted and talented pupils, EAL, looked after children (LAC)

- by the SEN Code of Practice graduated stages, i.e. Action, Action Plus, Statement

- by the four main types of SEN as specified in the SEN Code of Practice

- by the waves of intervention (Wave 2 and Wave 3).

The provision map needs to be kept under review each term, as SEN pupils progress and move through the SEN Code of Practice and CAF processes. It also needs to be reviewed annually, and this is best done in consultation with multi-agency professionals, key school staff, parents/carers and pupils. Some schools will hold a provision map day in the summer term to undertake this review with stakeholders and partners.

Developing a provision map

Six strategic stages are identified in developing a provision map. These are illustrated in Figure 2.5.

Table 2.2 provides a generic template for a provision map, which can be tailored and customised to suit the school context.

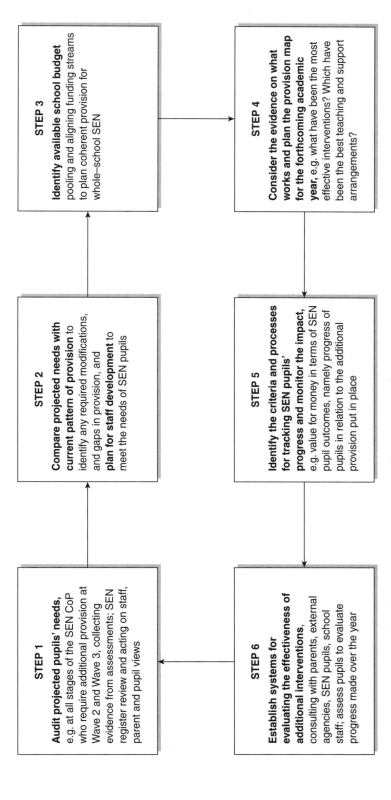

STEP 1

Audit projected pupils' needs, e.g. at all stages of the SEN CoP who require additional provision at Wave 2 and Wave 3, collecting evidence from assessments; SEN register review and acting on staff, parent and pupil views

STEP 2

Compare projected needs with current pattern of provision to identify any required modifications, and gaps in provision, and **plan for staff development** to meet the needs of SEN pupils

STEP 3

Identify available school budget pooling and aligning funding streams to plan coherent provision for whole–school SEN

STEP 4

Consider the evidence on what works and plan the provision map for the forthcoming academic year, e.g. what have been the most effective interventions? Which have been the best teaching and support arrangements?

STEP 5

Identify the criteria and processes for tracking SEN pupils' progress and monitor the impact, e.g. value for money in terms of SEN pupil outcomes, namely progress of pupils in relation to the additional provision put in place

STEP 6

Establish systems for evaluating the effectiveness of additional interventions, consulting with parents, external agencies, SEN pupils, school staff; assess pupils to evaluate progress made over the year

Figure 2.5 Stages in developing and reviewing an SEN provision map

Table 2.2 SEN provision map template

School name:							
			Term and year:				
Year group	Nature of SEN	Nature of intervention/ programme being delivered (and at which 'Wave')	Frequency and duration of intervention	Staff/pupil ratio (who is delivering and to how many pupils?)	Weekly cost in time (hours)	Total annual cost (£) and SEN budget source	Impact and outcomes
7							
8							
9							
10							
11							
12							
13							

Photocopiable:

Rita Cheminais' Handbook for New SENCOs © Rita Cheminais, 2010 (SAGE)

SENCOs will find it useful to combine the provision-mapping process with the Audit Commission's SEN/AEN Value for Money self-evaluation audit. The process of provision management and mapping enables the governing body, the head teacher and the SENCO to evaluate and analyse the cost-effectiveness and added value of the additional and different provision on improving outcomes for SEN pupils.

Examples of provision maps for SEN can be found in two National Strategies resources: the first is *Leading on Inclusion* (DfES, 2005a) and the second is *Maximising Progress* (DfES, 2005d: 17–18).

Making effective use of ICT to manage SEN systems

Information communication technology (ICT) is an invaluable management tool for SENCOs, designed to reduce the administrative burden of the SEN Code of Practice. By allowing SENCOs to work more efficiently, ICT enables them to devote more time to their strategic leadership role.

A SENCO has two choices:

1. To utilise the school's computerised management information system (MIS), i.e. CAPITA Children's Services SIMS modules that support SENCOs and incorporate IEP Writer 3, or Integris from RM, or Facility from SERCO, or e1 from Pearson.

2. To purchase a stand-alone ICT software package such as the popular SENCO Manager by Bluehills, who also produce Provision Map Writer, and IEP Pro. (Further information can be found at www.bluehills.co.uk/products)

SENCOs have valued using an electronic management information system to produce and maintain the SEN register, to maintain IEPs (if these are still in use), to generate standard letters from templates, as well as to produce and maintain the SEN provision map. SEN management software that pre-populates information is invaluable in saving SENCO time, and in ensuring they maintain a healthy work–life balance.

Whichever MIS a SENCO decides to use, it should:

- be easy to produce data and tables for reports

- present information in different formats

- be able to export and transport information from one electronic system to another

- have the flexibility to compare and analyse data, and produce this information as line graphs, bar and pie charts

- offer versatility in bringing together SEN assessment, monitoring and planning information

- be able to distribute SEN information to teachers across the school, to promote more immediate feedback and distribute ownership for SEN

- follow the principle of entering SEN information once, and using this many times.

SENCOs can also use ICT to access SEN information, advice and support at a local level via the local authority's SEN web pages, or nationally, by accessing the NASEN website, and the electronic SENCO forum hosted by the British Educational Communications and Technology Agency (Becta), where SENCOs can network with other SEN Coordinators nationally to share common interests and expertise and seek practical solutions to problems. The SENCO forum can be accessed at: http://inclusion.ngfl.gov.uk

Newly appointed SENCOs and suitably experienced SEN Coordinators can also access web-based SEN continuing professional development (CPD) materials, i.e. the National Strategies' Inclusion Development Programme (IDP), and SEN training resources on other websites such as the General Teaching Council (GTC), the Training and Development Agency for Schools (TDA), the Teacher Training Resource Bank (TTRB) and the National College for Leadership of Schools and Children's Services. General information on SEN can be found on the National Grid for Learning Inclusion website (http://inclusion.ngfl.gov.uk), which not only offers a vast array of practical advice on SEN and inclusion, but also on online communities.

Strategies for improving outcomes for pupils with SEN and/or disabilities

There have been a number of recent OFSTED and DfES reports which have explored what works well in inclusion and what improves outcomes for children with SEN and/or disabilities within mainstream schools and early years settings.

The following factors are a summary of improvements from these key official reports:

- having a welcoming 'can do' approach to SEN and inclusion

- having high expectations of what SEN pupils can achieve

- setting more challenging targets

- using good accurate assessment

- using a systematic analysis of SEN pupil-level attainment data to judge progress and inform provision

- adopting a robust self-evaluation of SEN provision which is linked to SEN pupils' outcomes

- having special and mainstream schools working in partnership to share teaching and curriculum expertise

- maintaining an effective use of ICT to enhance curriculum access

- adopting an inclusive pedagogy involving multi-method strategies, e.g. accelerated learning approaches; alternative methods of recording to enable SEN pupils to demonstrate their learning; collaborative and cooperative learning

- utilising SEN pupils' preferred learning style to get new information across, and to reinforce more difficult knowledge and concepts.

(See DfES, 2004c; Dyson et al., 2004; OFSTED, 2004a, 2005, 2006a.)

Additional interventions for pupils with SEN

The waves of intervention

The National Strategies promote the waves of intervention because they provide an inclusive approach to teaching and learning, which helps to minimise underachievement and close the attainment gap. The waves of intervention complement personalisation and the graduated response of the SEN Code of Practice. Although the SENCO will be familiar with the waves of intervention, they may find the following explanation valuable for use with those teaching colleagues who require clarification on how these relate to meeting the needs of SEN pupils.

Wave 1: Quality first teaching

This universal wave features high-quality inclusive teaching to meet the needs of the full diversity of pupils, including those with SEN, based on their prior learning. It focuses on moving pupils as learners from their current starting point to where they need to be and should be. This wave is reliant on making effective use of pupil-level attainment and well-being data in order to enable pupils to achieve the necessary progress. Quality first teaching is an entitlement for all pupils at all stages of the SEN Code of Practice. It also relates to the social and emotional aspects of learning (SEAL).

Wave 2: Quality first teaching plus additional time-limited, tailored intervention support programmes

This wave is designed to increase the rates of progress and secure good learning for groups of pupils, who may be falling behind, in order to get them back on track to meet or exceed national expectations. Wave 2 interventions usually take the form of a tight, structured programme of small group support, which is carefully targeted and delivered by teaching assistants or teachers. This support can be delivered outside, or within whole-class lessons as part of guided work. It also applies to additional interventions for pupils who require extra help in developing emotional, social and behavioural skills. Examples of Wave 2 interventions include: early literacy support (ELS), additional literacy support (ALS), further literacy support (FLS), Springboard Maths to support 'catch up', and the bridging units utilised in Year 7.

Wave 3: Quality first teaching plus increasingly individualised intervention programmes

Wave 3 expectations are to accelerate and maximise progress and to close performance gaps. These interventions may be delivered by a specialist SEN teacher or by highly trained teaching assistants, on a one-to-one or small group basis, to enable SEN pupils to meet very specific targets. The pupils receiving such interventions are likely to be at the Action, Action Plus or Statement stages. Wave 3 interventions are most effective when they operate intensively over a short, focused timescale of between eight to twenty weeks. Ideally, pupils on Wave 3 interventions should make on average at least twice the normal rate of progress. Examples of Wave 3 interventions include: Reading Recovery, PhonoGraphix, and Toe-by-Toe programmes.

SENCOs will need to evaluate these additional wave interventions to ensure that they are effective and work well. They will be expected to make an informed choice and impartial decision as to which programme gives the quickest impact and is good value for money. They should consult with SEN pupils to gain their views on the intervention programme. Where an additional intervention makes little impact, a SENCO needs to seek advice from the local authority consultants and from other SENCOs in order to find a more appropriate alternative.

The main impact measure used in relation to these additional interventions is ratio gain, i.e. the amount of progress pupils make, in months of reading or spelling age, divided by the number of months over which those gains were made. A ratio gain of one represents the normal rate of progress of all children over time: one month of reading or spelling age per month of chronological age.

Three National Strategy publications offer summaries and examples of a good range of the most effective intervention programmes, which SENCOs should make reference to: *Targeting Support, Leading on Inclusion* and *Maximising Progress* (DfEs, 2003a: 3–5; 2005a: 243ff; 2005d: 26–7).

Points to remember

- The key to successful strategic leadership is managing through others.
- Change is an ongoing developmental process.
- The governing body of the school has a statutory responsibility for SEN.
- SEN funding must add value to the work of the school.
- The SEN provision map is a strategic planning tool.
- Electronic SENCO management tools improve whole-school SEN
- communication.
- The use of evidence-based additional interventions with SEN pupils is key.

 Further activities

The following questions, focused on aspects covered in this chapter, meet the requirements of the National Award for Special Educational Needs Coordination, and support reflection and professional development:

1. How would you develop an agreed shared vision for the SEN whole school?

2. How could your role as SENCO be managed more efficiently to enable you to focus on the strategic aspects of leading SEN across the school?

3. The SEN governor is new to the role in school. As SENCO, what aspects of their role will you develop first and why?

4. What evidence would you present to the chair of governors to justify the decision to fund additional administrative time for the SENCO?

5. An aspect of SEN provision requires changing, but some staff are reluctant to make that change. As SENCO, explain how you will successfully manage this change process.

6. In order to know which interventions work best, describe the approaches you would adopt as SENCO to evaluate the effectiveness and impact of additional provision on SEN pupils' outcomes.

 Downloadable materials

For downloadable materials for this chapter visit www.sagepub.co.uk/ritacheminais

Figure 2.1 SEN development plan template

Figure 2.3 A model SEN leaflet for a parent

Figure 2.4 Template for reporting on SEN to the governing body

Table 2.1 SEN budget summary template

Table 2.2 SEN provision map template

Coordinating SEN provision

> This chapter covers the following TDA SENCO learning outcomes:
>
> - developing and using SEN systems – the SEN Framework and the DDA to:
>   - identify pupils with SEN and/or disabilities, including underachievers
>   - remove barriers to learning and participation
> - common entitlement, including:
>   - personalised learning and quality first teaching
>   - assessment for learning and pupil progress
> - using tools for collecting and analysing data
> - ensuring access by:
>   - applying for examination concessions for pupils
>   - addressing SEN and disability stereotyping and bullying
>   - coordinating the effective deployment of teaching assistants
>   - organising the transfer and transition of pupils with SEN and/ or disabilities.

Developing and using SEN systems – the SEN Framework and the DDA

Figure 3.1 illustrates the four key components relating to the coordination of SEN provision across the school. This chapter traces the SENCO journey, putting each piece of the jigsaw into place.

Identification of pupils who may have SEN and/or disabilities

The identification of pupils who may have a special educational need (SEN) requires the use of a range of methods to gather the necessary evidence that a child is functioning at a level below that of their peers of the same age.

A SENCO will need to liaise closely with a class teacher to collect evidence of a pupil's learning difficulties through:

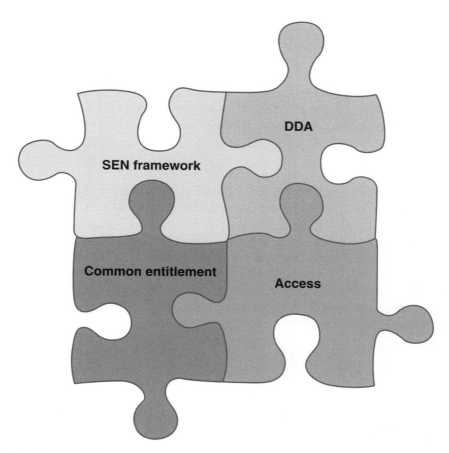

Figure 3.1 Framework for coordinating SEN provision

- observation of the child in lessons

- discussions with teachers, parents/carers of the pupil, and with the child (where appropriate), to gather qualitative information

- the completion of checklists

- samples of the pupil's work from across the curriculum

- attainment and progress data (both teacher assessment and test)

- attendance data and behaviour records

- the results from any screening or diagnostic assessments.

Assessment (diagnosis) of a pupil's special educational needs will assist the SENCO and class teacher in identifying the particular areas of learning difficulty; it provides a measure and record of the child's attainment and progress, which then informs the planning of additional interventions and provision. The use of such evidence supports any external professional observations and assessments, for example, those undertaken by the educational psychologist.

Screening a pupil on entry to school to establish a baseline of their strengths and needs provides an objective means of confirming a teacher's/SENCO's own observations in identifying those children who require more extensive assessment and examination. Examples of standardised screening tests include: the Group Reading Tests, the Cognitive Abilities Test (CAT) and the Suffolk Reading Scale. Standardised tests are uniformly developed, administered and scored.

Diagnostic assessment follows on from initial screening in order to provide more in-depth evidence on the particular aspects and severity of learning or behaviour in which the pupil is experiencing difficulties. Examples of diagnostic tests include: the Neale Analysis of Reading Ability, the Connors ADHD Rating Scale, the Aston Index and the British Picture Vocabulary Scale (BPVS).

A SENCO will need to build up a bank of basic screening and diagnostic assessment tools. They can seek advice on which to use by networking with other SENCOs locally, or asking the educational psychologist. The main companies who publish these tests are GL Assessment (www.gl-assessment.co.uk), Hodder Education (www.hoddertests.co.uk) and Pearson Education (www.pearson-uk.com).

High incidence SEN and practical approaches to meeting needs

Quality first teaching, as an aspect of personalised learning, is promoted by the National Strategies as being the most effective approach to utilise in meeting high incidence SEN in mainstream schools.

The National Strategies' Inclusion Development Programme (IDP) provides an essential resource to support teaching colleagues in meeting the needs of SEN pupils in mainstream schools and early years settings. This can be accessed at: http://national strategies.standards.dcsf.gov.uk/node/116691

The IDP covers the high incidence special educational needs: speech, language and communication needs (SLCN), including dyslexia; autistic spectrum disorders (ASD); moderate learning difficulties (MLD); and behavioural, emotional and social difficulties (BESD). It offers guidance on effective classroom strategies, and signposts teachers to other sources of information.

A SENCO will need to signpost teaching and learning support staff to the IDP, in addition to delivering a session on this resource to all staff, to introduce them to the wealth of materials available which focus on identifying and removing barriers to learning.

Identifying and addressing SEN pupil underachievement

Underachievement refers to a mismatch between current levels of attainment and potential, which results in a pupil not achieving the national expectation at the end of a key stage. Pupils are considered to be underachieving when standards in attainment, pupil progress or attendance fall below the national averages. High levels of school exclusions, pupil absences, truancy, poor behaviour or high rates of pupil mobility are other indicators of underachievement. Recent government statistics on SEN found that these pupils represented one of the vulnerable underachieving groups of children and young people.

The causes of underachievement

The main causes of underachievement are summarised in Table 3.1.

Strategies to address underachievement

The government has invested heavily in addressing underachievement among vulnerable groups of children and young people, which includes those with SEN and/ or disabilities – for example, through the Children's Centres initiative, extended services, catch-up programmes, summer school activities, anti-bullying strategies and improving the transfer between primary and secondary schools.

How the SENCO can check if pupils with SEN and/or disabilities are underachieving

Undertaking work scrutiny and the sampling of SEN pupils' work across the curriculum are valuable ways of identifying potential underachievement.

A SENCO should look for:

- variations in the presentation of written work – legibility, untidiness

- unfinished pieces of work and homework

- poor written expression and work lacking clarity or sense

- inaccurate work with misunderstandings and irrelevance

- poor quality diagrams

- patchy or no evidence of transference of learning from additional literacy or numeracy interventions across the curriculum

- an erratic performance from subject to subject, and/or over time.

A SENCO needs to seek a pupil's views about the variation, and cross-check these with subject teachers' or class teachers' perceptions and comments. Work scrutiny needs to be supported by other contextual evidence relating to pupil attendance, ability, dual or multiple exceptionality, behaviour, emotional well-being, and the nature of SEN and disability. The entire process will help to identify SEN pupil underperformance, the reasons for it, and the strategies to address it.

Some pupils with disabilities may underachieve as a result of not having the appropriate resources to access the curriculum, or because teachers don't give them extra

Table 3.1   Causes of underachievement

School factors	Classroom factors
• Inappropriate curriculum • Ineffective reward system • Lack of flexibility in timetabling • Inconsistently applied behaviour policy	• Mismatch between delivery of the curriculum and a pupil's preferred learning style • Lessons too long • Poor differentiation • Lack of challenge • Unclear instructions and explanations • Poorly paced and structured lessons • Passive learning environment • Inappropriate groupings and seating arrangements
Family circumstances	**Within-child factors**
• Family break-up • Family illness • Family bereavement • Neglect • Abuse	• Tiredness • Low self-esteem • Lack of self-confidence • Poor social skills • Sensory or physical impairment • Specific learning difficulty

time to complete tasks. Therefore, it cannot be assumed that all pupils with disabilities necessarily have inherent special educational needs.

Removing barriers to learning and participation

The SEN Code of Practice (DfES, 2001b: para. 5.6) and the government publication *Removing Barriers to Achievement* (DfES, 2004d: para. 2.1) both identify what causes pupils with SEN and/or disabilities to experience barriers to learning and participation.

OFSTED, in their HMI report *Special Educational Needs and Disability* (2004a), found from inspection evidence that some SEN pupils face barriers to participation and achievement, due to inaccessible premises and a shortage of sufficient adult support.

A SENCO needs to ensure that teachers and learning support staff are aware of these barriers; are able to identify them within the classroom; and know what approaches to utilise in order to remove or minimise these.

There is an excellent table in the Primary National Strategy (DfES, 2004h: 39–42) resource, *Learning and Teaching for Children with Special Educational Needs in the Primary Years*, which provides practical strategies for removing barriers to learning. The Key Stage 3 booklet, Part 1 in *Maximising Progress* (DfES, 2005c), also provides a comprehensive list of practical approaches a SENCO can advise class and subject teachers to adopt in order to ensure pupils with SEN and disabilities reach their optimum potential.

Appropriate strategies to remove barriers to learning and participation

The government promotes personalised learning as being an effective approach to adopt for all pupils, including those with SEN and/or disabilities. Similarly, the National Strategies' Inclusion Development Programme (IDP) emphasises and reinforces a generic strengthening of quality first teaching and personalised learning in order to meet a diversity of high incidence SEN in mainstream schools, as well as helping to address any underachievement.

The SEN Code of Practice referred to personalisation indirectly when it stated:

> Effective management, school ethos and the learning environment, curricular, pastoral and discipline arrangements can help prevent some special educational needs arising and minimise others. (DfES, 2001b: 47, 62, paras 5.18, 6.18)

Common entitlement

Personalised learning

Personalised learning embraces every aspect of school life including teaching and learning strategies; ICT; curriculum choice, organisation and timetabling; and assessment arrangements and relationships with the local community. It takes a highly structured and responsive approach by tailoring and matching teaching and learning around the way different learners learn, in order to meet individual needs, interests and aptitudes and enable every pupil to reach their optimum potential.

Paragraphs 3.1 and 3.2 in *Removing Barriers to Achievement* (DfES, 2004d) illustrate how teachers can deliver personalised learning. A SENCO may find it helpful to disseminate this information to those teaching staff who require additional support and guidance in relation to this aspect.

In 2008 the DCSF published *Personalised Learning*, which provided a useful framework comprised of nine interrelated features making up a pedagogy of personalised learning (2008b: 54). SENCOs can play a key role in supporting other colleagues in meeting the needs of pupils with SEN and/or disabilities through modelling personalised learning approaches.

Quality first teaching

Effective teaching for children with SEN and/or disabilities shares most of the characteristics of effective teaching for all pupils. Quality first teaching (QFT) for all pupils makes up the daily repertoire of teaching strategies and techniques that ensures pupils' progression in learning. It includes guided work for small groups that is integrated into whole-class teaching where work is pitched at appropriate levels for differing groups within a class; and curriculum differentiation where the teacher stages work by level of support, open-tasking, and extension, enrichment and enhancement activities.

(See DCSF, 2008b: 12 for further information about the features of quality first teaching – a SENCO may wish to signpost staff to view this information.)

As part of a SENCO's role in coordinating and monitoring the provision for pupils with SEN and/or disabilities across the school, in partnership with the senior leadership team, they would expect to see the following aspects of QFT in practice:

- lessons differentiated and personalised to match learners' needs, which make reasonable adjustments for those pupils with SEN and/or disabilities

- pupils as active participants and cooperative learners in the learning process

- staff having high enough expectations of SEN pupils

- learning which builds on prior knowledge and understanding

- links made to and a transfer of learning across the curriculum

- teachers using a range of teaching approaches

- an effective use of ICT to enhance curriculum access and learning opportunities.

Understanding assessment for learning

Assessment for learning (AfL) is defined as the process of seeking and interpreting evidence for use by pupils and their teachers to decide how far pupils have reached in their learning, where they need to go next, and how best to get there. AfL, as part of personalised learning, is essential because it helps to guide classroom practice for all pupils, including those with SEN and/or disabilities. A SENCO will need to ensure that class/subject teachers are engaging these pupils in assessing their own learning and progress, wherever possible.

The National Strategies have further strengthened AfL by introducing assessing pupil progress (APP). This process entails class/subject teachers tracking the progress of at least three pupils in a class periodically, over a year, to ensure that they are on track and making the appropriate rate of progress and not falling behind or underachieving.

A SENCO will be able to check if AfL and APP are enabling teachers to identify:

- what is helping or hindering pupils with SEN and/or disabilities to access and participate in the curriculum and learning

- the impact of teaching and learning support on SEN pupils' learning

- the strengths and talents SEN pupils have

- any gaps, misconceptions or misunderstandings in SEN pupils' learning

- the appropriate level of challenge to set in relation to SEN pupils' targets

- what the views of SEN pupils are in relation to their learning and progress.

A SENCO may find the table in DfES, 2005d: 15 very useful to share with teaching and learning support staff, as it offers a range of strategies to support assessment for learning.

The progress of SEN pupils

SENCOs should refer to the SEN Code of Practice (2001b: paras 5.42, 6.49) which holistically describes adequate progress for pupils with SEN. This is important information for a SENCO to share with teaching and learning support staff in relation to raising expectations about the progress of pupils with SEN and/or disabilities.

The DCSF/National Strategies (2009f) clarify what constitutes good progress for pupils with SEN in English, mathematics and science. There is an emphasis on three key principles:

1. High expectations are key to securing good progress.

2. Age and prior attainment inform expectations of pupil progress.

3. Moderation is key to improving the reliability of teacher assessment.

The government's expectation for learners identified as having SEN, who are working within age-related expectations, is that they should make at least two levels of progress across a Key Stage.

OFSTED (2006a) confirmed that good progress for pupils with SEN was usually a gain of two National Curriculum levels or two P levels, dependent on a pupil's starting point across a Key Stage.

Two levels of progress equate to six sub-levels and 12 points in National Curriculum terms. Pupils on average are expected to achieve one point in a term and one sub-level in two terms. One value added point is equivalent to one sixth of a level or one term's progress. (Value added looks at attainment as well as progress.)

Progress measured on the basis of age and prior attainment enables more objective comparisons and judgements to be made as to what constitutes good progress for pupils with SEN. This information also helps to inform the setting of more stretching targets for SEN pupils.

The DCSF/National Strategies' *Progression Guidance* can be accessed at: www.standards.dcsf.gov.uk/nationalstrategies/inclusion/specialeducationalneeds

Table 3.2 Good and outstanding progress for learners with SEN/LDD

Year Group	P level/NC level	Good	Outstanding
Year 5			
Who at the end of Year 2 achieved	P1 – P3	One level gain	One or more level gain
	P4 – P7	More than 1 level	More than 2 level gains
	P8	Level gain to lower levels of NC Level 2	Gain to NC Level 2 or more
	NC Level 1	Level gain to lower levels of NC Level 3	Gain to NC Level 3 or more
	NC Level 2	Level gain to lower levels of NC Level 4	Gain to NC Level 4 or more
	NC Level 3	Level gain to lower levels of NC Level 5	Two level gains or more
	NC Level 4	Level gain to lower levels of NC Level 6	Lower NC Level 6 or more
Year 8			
Who at the end of Year 6 achieved	P1 – P3	One sub-level gain	One or more level gain
	P4 – P7	One level gain	More than 1 level gain
	P8	Level gain to NC Level 1	More than 1 level gain
	NC Level 1	Level gain to NC Level 2	More than 1 level gain
	NC Level 2	Level gain to NC Level 3	More than 1 level gain
	NC Level 3	Level gain to NC Level 4	More than 1 level gain
	NC Level 4	More than 1 level gain	More than 2 level gains
	NC Level 5	Two level gains	More than 3 level gains
	NC Level 6	More than 2 level gains	More than 2+ level gains
Year 10			
Who at the end of Year 6 achieved	P1 – P3	One sub-level gain	One or more level gain
	P4 – P7	One level gain	More than 1 level gain
	P8	Level gain to NC Level 1	More than 1 level gain
	NC Level 1	Level gain to NC Level 2	More than 1 level gain
	NC Level 2	Level gain to NC Level 3	More than 1 level gain
	NC Level 3	Level gain to lower levels of NC Level 5	Level gain to NC Level 5 or more
	NC Level 4	Level gain to lower levels of NC Level 6	Level gain to NC Level 6 or more
	NC Level 5	Level gain to lower levels of NC Level 7	Level gain to lower levels of NC Level 7 or more
	NC Level 6	More than 1 level gain	More than 2 level gains

Photocopiable:

Table 3.2 provides a guide to what constitutes good and outstanding progress for pupils with SEN at the primary and secondary phases of education, from Key Stage 2 through to Key Stage 4.

SENCOs will find it useful to use Table 3.2 in conjunction with Annex B of OFSTED's (2004a: 25) report, *Special Educational Needs and Disability*, where supporting criteria for evaluating whether pupils with SEN make good progress in relation to their starting points, compared with pupils with similar difficulties and circumstances, are offered. For example:

- At least 80% of pupils make the nationally expected gains of two levels at Key Stage 2 and one level at Key Stage 3.

- 78% of pupils who begin Key Stage 2 at level 1 in English achieve level 3 by the end of Key Stage 2.

- At least 34% of pupils below level 2 in English in Year 7 make a one-level gain by the end of Key Stage 3 and 55% of pupils at level 2 make this gain.

- Pupils withdrawn for substantial literacy support make an average of double the normal rate of progress.

- The attendance of pupils with special needs is good (above 92%) and unauthorised absence is low.

The revised OFSTED inspection schedule for September 2009 also provides clear criteria for judging the quality of SEN pupils' learning and progress (2009: 14). It is well worth sharing this with teachers and learning support staff.

OFSTED inspectors during their inspections will be examining SEN pupil progress data over the last three years within schools to explore whether these children are reaching challenging targets.

The DCSF (2009i), in their analysis of children with special educational needs progression between Key Stage 2 and Key Stage 4, found that:

- pupils with statements of SEN generally made more progress than those pupils at School Action Plus

- pupils at School Action Plus made the least progress

- pupils with SEN born earlier in the academic year performed better at Key Stages 2 and 4 than those SEN pupils born in the summer (August)

- pupils born in the summer (August) at Key Stage 2 were 1.5 times more likely to have SEN, and at Key Stage 4, 1.2 times more likely to have SEN.

A SENCO needs to consider the progress of the SEN pupils in their school, in light of these national findings, particularly the summer birth issue and the School Action Plus issue.

Further detailed information about the rates of SEN pupil progress can be found in the DCSF (2009i) publication with accompanying data annexes, which can be downloaded at: www.dcsf.gov.uk/rsgateway/DB/STA/t000851/index.shtml

P levels

Where there are pupils working below National Curriculum level 1, the use of the P levels enables schools to measure progress, set targets and evaluate the impact of their provision for these SEN pupils. Table 3.3 provides a point score conversion for these levels, which will assist SENCOs, core subject coordinators and class teachers to measure the progress of pupils with more complex SEN.

The P levels are differentiated performance criteria for assessing the attainment of those SEN pupils aged between 5 and 16, who are working below National Curriculum level 1. There are P levels in every National Curriculum subject, including Religious Education (RE) and Personal, Social and Health Education (PSHE). P1 to P3 relate to the early levels of general attainment and P4 to P8 relate to subject attainment.

The P levels support summative assessment at the end of an academic year or Key Stage. They help to track and identify linear and lateral pupil progress. They provide a best-fit judgement on SEN pupil performance, as a pupil may not demonstrate every element of a P-level descriptor.

QCA (now known as QCDA) produced a DVD pack in 2005, *Using the P Scales,* to support teacher moderation of P levels in English, mathematics and science. This is available from: www.qcda.org.uk

In addition, there is a series of recently revised curriculum P level booklets, which provide guidance on how to respond to pupil learning needs; how to modify the programmes of study; how to improve access to the specific curriculum subject; and examples of activities that pupils can do in Key Stage 1, Key Stage 2 and Key Stage 3. These booklets can be downloaded from the QCDA website.

Using tools for collecting and analysing data

Analysing and using SEN pupil-level data

The effective use of data helps to improve teaching and learning and support the development of a strategic approach to the management of SEN. According to the National Strategies, data collection and analysis are essential elements in developing a more 'forensic' approach to removing barriers to learning, raising expectations and supporting the setting of realistic and stretching targets for SEN pupils.

The analysis of SEN pupil-level data can provide a deeper understanding of the performance of individual and groups of SEN pupils over time and help to inform the appropriate additional interventions required to ensure SEN pupils make the necessary two levels of progress across a Key Stage, including securing the progression of those SEN pupils with significant learning difficulties and/or disabilities who are operating at very low levels of the National Curriculum and P levels, and who are likely to make one level or smaller-stepped progress over a Key Stage.

Table 3.3 P level point-score values

P level point score	P levels and sub-levels	Range for converting point scores back into P levels
0.5	P1i	>=0 and <0.6
0.7	P1ii	>=0.6 and <0.8
0.9	P2i	>=0.8 and <1
1.1	P2ii	>=1 and <1.2
1.3	P3i	>=1.2 and <1.4
1.5	P3ii	>=1.4 and <1.6
2	P4	>=1.6 and <2.4
3	P5	>=2.4 and <3.4
4	P6	>=3.4 and <4.4
5	P7	>=4.4 and <5.4
6	P8	>=5.4 and <6.4
7	L1i	>=6.4 and <8
9	L1ii	>=8 and <10
11	L1iii	>=10 and <12

SEN data analysis also offers SENCOs a better understanding of the impact of the additional and different types of extra interventions and provision on SEN pupils' progress. Effective strategic analysis and interpretation of robust SEN data can help to inform teaching and learning at the classroom level. SENCOs need to reflect on the following aspects, which are essential to using and analysing SEN pupil-level data:

- the criteria being used to determine whether SEN pupils are underachieving

- the strategies and approaches being used to address any SEN pupil under-achievement and to narrow the attainment gap

- the key national indicators and SEN data sets essential to monitoring SEN pupil progress

- the systems and approaches being used across the school to assess, target set and evaluate SEN pupils' rates of progress

- what constitutes good progress for SEN pupils within the school, and takes account of linear and lateral progress

- the effectiveness of the SENCO working with subject leaders and Key Stage coordinators in the school to jointly analyse and interpret SEN pupil-level data in order to identify strengths and gaps in subject coverage, or aspects of a subject that require further development and improvement.

Why analyse SEN data?

A SENCO, in partnership with the assessment coordinator in school, will need to interrogate SEN pupil-level data in RAISEonline and Fischer Family Trust (FFT), in addition to the information in their own internal data sets, in order to:

- contribute evidence to the school's OFSTED self-evaluation form (SEF) on how well pupils with SEN and/or disabilities are progressing

- evaluate the impact of additional intervention programmes and in-house provision on SEN pupils' outcomes, and in relation to providing good value for money

- evaluate the progress towards meeting the targets set for SEN pupils

- make informed decisions about the deployment of SEN resources

- evaluate the support and interventions provided by external agencies, including the impact of any extended school activities SEN pupils have accessed

- identify trends over three years

- compare the school's SEN pupil performance with that of similar schools, locally and regionally

- identify any gaps existing in SEN provision

- identify any SEN pupils who may be underachieving.

What data should a SENCO be using and analysing?

A SENCO needs to gather qualitative as well as quantitative evidence to gain a secure view about the progress of SEN pupils. The following questions can provide some useful prompts:

1. What does SEN pupil data tracking say about their progress?

2. What are the SEN pupils' views about their progress?

3. What are the views of staff and external professionals about SEN pupils' progress?

4. What do observations from lessons indicate about pupils' progress?

5. What does the scrutiny of SEN pupils' work across the curriculum indicate about their progress?

A SENCO will need to give careful consideration to the type of SEN data that will be most useful to collect and analyse, and how and when that data should be used. The following list suggests the types of data a SENCO could analyse:

- contextualised value-added (CVA) data, which look at what is expected of each SEN pupil in relation to progress in the context of a range of factors such as: prior attainment, SEN status, free school meals (FSM), LAC, EAL, ethnicity, gender, age, mobility, economic deprivation, summer births and question level on SATs

- value-added data which compare each SEN pupil's result with the median result for all pupils nationally with the same average point score at an earlier Key Stage, i.e. the difference between a pupil's actual result and the expected result at the end of a Key Stage

- attendance data, particularly persistent absenteeism data and the absence of SEN pupils who are taking holidays in term time

- exclusions data (fixed term and permanent exclusions)

- ECM well-being outcomes data

- rewards and sanctions data

- extended services data – which activities SEN pupils access and how frequently

- health and emotional well-being data from annual surveys such as the Tell Us Survey, the Health Related Behaviour Questionnaire (HRBQ), the Pupil Attitude to Self and School (PASS) and the QCDA emotional and behavioural development scales.

Analysis of the SEN pupil-level data should help to demonstrate the impact additional provision is making; identify any gaps in provision; and see if particular groups of SEN pupils are making better progress than others.

Understanding RAISEonline and Fischer Family Trust data

RAISEonline and Fischer Family Trust are two data packages used by schools, local authorities, school improvement partners and OFSTED inspectors. Both packages use contextual data gathered from the School Census within their CVA models to compare attainment and progress linked to levels of interventions for pupils at School Action or School Action Plus Stage, and for pupils with a statement of SEN.

SENCOs are expected to be able to use and analyse SEN pupil-level data in both of the data packages, as well as interpret and compare their school-level SEN data with the national data sets for SEN/LDD, which can be found on the SEN/LDD area of the DCSF Standards website (www.standards.dfes.gov.uk).

Online guidance is provided for RAISEonline and Fischer Family Trust, which can be downloaded from the respective websites: www.raiseonline.org and www. fischertrust.org

A SENCO would be advised to book a session with the school's assessment coordinator and/or the head teacher to take them through the operational aspects of accessing different data sets within each package, if they are new to this aspect of their role. In addition, the local authority data team or school improvement team can often provide training on the use of these data packages. Another option is for a SENCO to spend half a day with another local skilled SENCO who is conversant with both data packages.

SENCOs may find two National Strategies resources particularly useful in giving further background information about using and analysing data. The first is *Leading on Inclusion* (DfES, 2005a, Section 2), and the second is *Maximising Progress* (DfES, 2005c).

Ensuring access

Examination access arrangements for pupils with SEN and/or disabilities

A SENCO is responsible for liaising with and informing the school's examination officer and/or assessment coordinator of all the pupils with SEN and/or disabilities requiring access arrangements for the end of Key Stage 2 and for the Key Stage 4 external examinations.

Pupils eligible for test and examination access arrangements include:

- pupils with a statement of special educational needs

- pupils at School Action or School Action Plus Stage

- pupils who require alternative access arrangements owing to a disability (which may or may not give rise to a special educational need)

- pupils who are unable to sit and work for extensive periods of time because of a disability, or because of their behavioural, emotional or social difficulties (BESD)

- pupils with English as a second language (EAL) and those who have limited fluency in English.

The access arrangements for Key Stage 4 are very similar to those for Key Stage 2 which cover:

- additional time allowed of 25% and 100% for pupils with a visual impairment or long-term hearing loss

- the early opening of test papers to enable adaptations or enlargements to be made. Where pupils with visual impairments require Braille tests or large-print versions, the test papers can be opened two days in advance. For modified versions of test papers, these may be opened one day in advance

- special consideration, which is granted to pupils whose test performance is affected by extremely distressing circumstances, for example: pupils who have experienced a death in the family or that of a close friend; a serious and disruptive domestic crisis; the terminal illness or major surgery of a pupil or close family member; or other major, unpredicted disruptions

Table 3.4 Timetable for applications for examination and test access arrangements

Month	Activity
November prior to testing until 1 March of the year of testing	Apply for early opening of papers and additional time application
Mid-April of the year of testing	Notification of decisions concerning applications for access arrangements
May 21 of year of testing	Deadline for special consideration application
Before the end of June of the year of testing	QCDA will have made their decision as to whether the school is eligible for the special considerations applied for

- readers – these are only for those pupils who regularly receive reading support. Usually a teaching assistant, these are used on a one-to-one basis.

- amanuenses – a scribe (writing assistant) who writes out pupils' dictated answers, and is used where they are part of pupils' normal classroom practice

- the use of word processors and technical electrical aids, e.g. voice-activated software (only when these are used as part of pupils' normal classroom practice)

- the use of communicators and signers for pupils who use British Sign Language and lip reading

- the use of real objects/apparatus such as mathematical shapes

- rest breaks for pupils who have difficulty concentrating or who suffer fatigue

- the use of prompters such as teaching assistants to help keep pupils on task who experience severe attention problems.

Table 3.4 provides SENCOs with a timetable to remind them of the deadlines for making and gaining access arrangements.

Applications for access arrangements are made electronically by the school's examination officer/assessment coordinator.

Supporting evidence for additional time

Pupils with a statement of SEN are automatically eligible for an additional length of time of 25% at the discretion of the school. SENCOs will have to support additional time requests with relevent evidence, i.e. the outcomes of standardised testing using approved tests recognised by the QCDA. These tests have to be up to date, fully standardised and age-appropriate, with a ceiling level at or above the pupil's chronological age. Only standardised scores must be given on the application form for up to 25% additional time, along with the name of the test used and its publisher. The

QCDA provide a comprehensive list of standardised tests that SENCOs can use to supply a reading age, a comprehension age and a verbal reasoning and non-verbal reasoning age, which can be accessed at: www.qcda.gov.uk/accessarrangements

SENCOs will also require the most up-to-date version of the QCDA (2009b) booklet *Assessment and Reporting Arrangements*.

Addressing stereotyping and bullying related to SEN and disability

Bullying creates a barrier to children's learning and prevents them from leading a fulfilled and happy life. The DCSF (2009i) found that pupils with a learning difficulty were more likely to be bullied than those pupils without SEN. The reasons for SEN pupils being a target for bullying and experiencing personal distress was as a result of them:

- being viewed as 'different' and therefore an easy target for bullying

- not realising they were actually being bullied, with incidents therefore going unreported

- having limited communication skills and thus finding it difficult to tell an adult that they were being bullied

- being more isolated as a result of having fewer friends than other peers

- forgetting to report a bullying incident immediately because of their poor memory skills

- being a dual-placement pupil who was spending time in a mainstream school for some part of the week, and therefore being more exposed to bullying from their mainstream peers.

A definition of bullying

Bullying is defined as behaviour by an individual or a group which is repeated over time and which intentionally hurts another individual or group either physically or emotionally.

The Anti-bullying Alliance has a pupil-friendly definition of bullying: 'People doing nasty or unkind things to you on purpose more than once, which it is difficult to stop'.

Pupils with SEN and disabilities have the same rights and entitlements to be safe and free from bullying as all other children and young people. The Disability Equality Duty is designed to eliminate harassment and discrimination through a school's Disability Equality Scheme. The Disability Discrimination Act also requires schools to promote positive attitudes towards the disabled, to challenge stereotypical views, to make reasonable adjustments and to ensure fair treatment.

The role of a SENCO in relation to bullying

A SENCO plays a crucial role in securing the well-being of pupils with SEN and disabilities, in that they:

- act as a champion for inclusion

- raise staff awareness through training on disability equality

- make valuable contributions to the development and review of a school's anti-bullying and behaviour policies

- promote the participation of pupils with SEN and disability in any consultations on behaviour and bullying in school

- ensure BESD pupils receive additional support and interventions to enable them to learn about respect and tolerance for others' differences

- ensure SEN pupils who are the victims of bullying receive the necessary support and interventions to help them deal with it and give them coping strategies to tackle bullying in the future

- monitor the impact of anti-bullying interventions for individual pupils with SEN and/or disabilities.

Teaching assistants and midday welfare assistants can also play an important role in preventing pupils with SEN and/or disabilities being bullied, particularly outside the classroom at break and lunchtimes, and when these pupils are undertaking extended school activities.

Table 3.5 offers some recommended strategies at a whole-school level and also at a classroom level to prevent stereotyping and the bullying of SEN pupils from occurring.

Coordinating the effective deployment of teaching assistants

OFSTED commented:

> Support by teaching assistants can be vital, but the organisation of it can mean pupils have insufficient opportunity to improve their understanding, skills and independence. (2004a: 5)

The role of teaching assistants (TAs) is more effective when they work in partnership with teachers on joint planning for the inclusion and engagement of SEN pupils in lessons. In order to maximise the full potential of teaching assistants, teachers need to inform them of the expected learning objectives and outcomes and of the activities and tasks planned, well in advance of lessons.

The effectiveness of additional TA support is dependent on a good two-way and open communication existing between the teacher and the teaching assistant, who both need to keep the SENCO informed about the progress of SEN pupils and of any barriers to learning and participation they may face.

The role of a SENCO in coordinating the effective deployment of teaching assistants

A SENCO's role in coordinating the effective deployment of learning support entails:

- producing a clear, up-to-date job description for teaching assistants

- recruiting, inducting, training and managing the team of teaching assistants, with the support of the senior leadership team

- planning the allocation of in-class teaching assistant support across the school and the curriculum to meet the needs of SEN pupils, in light of the SEN budget available

- identifying the teaching assistants and other additional supporting adults e.g. SEN teachers, learning mentor, following provision mapping, who will deliver targeted Wave 2 and Wave 3 additional intervention programmes

- devising timetables for teaching assistants and other support staff, and keeping these under review

- planning the annual programme for learning support team meetings

- negotiating non-contact time for teaching assistants to enable them to differentiate curriculum materials in school time, and also to liaise with subject/class teachers and other professionals from external agencies

- providing access to relevant ongoing professional development for TAs and others in the learning support team

- providing coaching and mentoring to newly appointed teaching assistants and other new staff joining the learning support team

- monitoring and evaluating the effectiveness and impact of teaching assistants' support and interventions

- undertaking annual appraisals and professional development reviews with teaching assistants, which link to the National Occupational Standards for supporting teaching and learning.

Figure 3.2 provides a model job description for a teaching assistant, working in a twenty-first-century school. This can be tailored or customised to suit the context of the school or other educational setting.

Table 3.5 Practical strategies to prevent the stereotyping and bullying of SEN pupils in schools

Whole-school strategies	Classroom strategies
<ul><li>Positive images of successful disabled people are displayed</li><li>School drama productions include disabled pupils, and have a theme on disability in some productions</li><li>School assembly on inclusion has a focus disability</li><li>Pupils with SEN have an opportunity to meet with the governors to present their views</li><li>Parents of disabled pupils can contribute their knowledge and expertise on disability at staff INSET</li><li>A consistent system for recording bullying incidents is in place which is followed by all staff</li><li>Robust whole-school behaviour and anti-bullying policies are in place which are kept under regular review and involve key stakeholders, including SEN pupils</li><li>A good range of extended school activities is fully accessible to those with disabilities, including wheelchair users</li><li>An anti-bullying week takes place annually</li><li>The school has a Quiet Zone in school for pupils who need a safe haven</li><li>There is a system of peer supporters and playground buddies operating</li><li>Circle Time provides a forum for discussing bullying</li><li>Anti-bullying interventions are evaluated for effectiveness</li><li>Visible staff are around school and out at break times and lunchtimes</li><li>Counselling provision is available in school and as an electronic service for pupils to access in order to report and discuss bullying issues</li></ul>	<ul><li>The SEAL bullying-related materials are utilised</li><li>Alternative methods of recording are available to enable SEN pupils to report bullying and their feelings in a range of ways</li><li>SEN pupils' views are listened to by staff</li><li>Staff know which agencies to seek further information from about anti-bullying and SEN pupils</li><li>The DDA and Disability Equality Duties are displayed in a pupil-friendly format within a classroom</li><li>Staff work in partnership with special school staff to further develop their inclusive practice and knowledge about the needs of disabled pupils</li><li>Positive images of disability are promoted across the curriculum</li><li>Each class has a nominated pupil anti-bullying representative</li><li>Class teachers use three positive statements for every one negative statement</li><li>Teachers analyse SEN pupil-level attendance data to look for any correlation between absences by these pupils from school and bullying incidents, and follow up on any issues.</li></ul>

There are two excellent resources for SENCOs in relation to coordinating, managing and monitoring the effectiveness of teaching assistants (or learning support assistants in the secondary phase). These are as follows: *Effective Leadership* (DfES, 2006a, Section B: 11–13, 24) and *Maximising Progress* (DfES, 2005e, Part 3: 19–22).

The latter includes an excellent monitoring table (p. 21) which a SENCO could download and either use to monitor TAs working in the classroom, or give to senior leadership staff when they have a focus on monitoring the impact of additional supporting adults.

In effectively supported lessons, teaching assistants ensure that SEN pupils are clear about:

- what is to be learned

- how this links with what they already know and with their targets

- what they are expected to do as independent learners in the lesson

- what they should recognise they have learned by the end of the lesson

- what the next steps in their learning will be.

SENCO evaluation on the deployment of teaching assistants

SENCOs may find Table 3.6 helpful in making judgements about the effective deployment of TAs. It mirrors the type of criteria that OFSTED would make judgements against.

SENCOs will need to gather the views of SEN pupils, teachers receiving in-class support from teaching assistants, and from the TA themselves, on their learning support work in the academic year. Figure 3.3 provides a generic survey that can be completed by all three stakeholders. The findings can help to inform whether a SENCO needs to make any necessary changes to the deployment of teaching assistants.

SENCOs need to consider the following questions:

- How are teaching assistants being actively engaged in an SEN policy review, SEN development planning and provision mapping?

- How will you ensure that class and subject teachers support teaching assistants in enabling SEN pupils to transfer what they have learned in targeted intervention programmes across the curriculum?

- How are teaching assistants actively engaged in monitoring the impact of their support and interventions?

The transfer and transition of pupils with SEN and/or disabilities

The transfer from primary to secondary school can be a particularly stressful period in an SEN pupil's educational career, causing some Year 6 children to become anxious,

Job Title: Teaching Assistant supporting teaching and learning

Responsible to: SEN Coordinator

Main Purpose: To work with individual and small groups of SEN pupils, under the direction of the class/subject teacher, in order to promote the inclusion of SEN pupils in a mainstream class, and to provide support for teaching and personalised learning.

Main Duties:

Supporting SEN pupils' personalised learning

- Support pupils' learning across the curriculum, tailoring support to match learners' needs
- Support pupils to become independent, cooperative and collaborative learners
- Support pupils' access to learning through the effective use of ICT
- Contribute to assessing pupils' progress, and support them in reviewing their own learning
- Identify and remove barriers to pupils' learning
- Adapt and customise curriculum materials
- Support teacher planning

Meeting pupils' additional needs

- Support the learning and emotional well-being of a diversity of SEN pupils, including those with dual and/or multiple exceptionalities
- Promote pupils' well-being (ECM outcomes)
- Contribute to the management of SEN pupils' behaviour
- Support the delivery of Wave 2 and Wave 3 interventions in literacy and numeracy and monitor their impact
- Support pupils with SEN and/or disabilities to access extended school activities

Providing pastoral support

- Promote SEN pupils' well-being and resilience
- Safeguard the welfare of SEN pupils
- Support the transition and transfer of SEN pupils
- Act as a 'champion' and advocate for children with special educational needs

Supporting the wider work of the school

- Comply with school policies and procedures related to child protection and safeguarding, health and safety, inclusion and SEN, Disability Equality Duty, Information Sharing and Data Protection
- Contribute to the school's improvement planning and self-evaluation processes
- Support teachers in the administration of examinations and tests
- Contribute to maintaining pupil records
- Assist teachers with the display of pupils' work and achievements
- Contribute to the school's extended services core offer
- Escort and supervise SEN pupils on educational visits and out-of-school activities
- Contribute to, and support, the Common Assessment Framework (CAF) process

Working with colleagues

- Support and maintain collaborative, productive working relationships with school staff and professionals from external agencies
- Contribute to and support the work of the learning support team in school
- Liaise with pupils, their parents/carers, teachers and practitioners from external agencies to support pupils' learning and well-being
- Take responsibility in developing your own continuing professional development
- Undertake any other duties commensurate with the post, as allocated by the head teacher

Figure 3.2 Teaching assistant job description

Photocopiable:

Table 3.6 Evaluating the deployment of teaching assistants

Grade	Evidence descriptor
Outstanding (1)	• Teaching assistants are well-directed to support learning. • They make a significant contribution in very effectively supporting SEN pupils' learning and well-being. • They understand the next steps SEN pupils need to take, and provide a wide range of learning support activities.
Good (2)	• Teaching assistants are well-deployed and are effective in what they do. • Teaching assistants relate well to the SEN pupils they support and expect them to work hard.
Satisfactory (3)	• Teaching assistants are utilised adequately. • They are not effective in supporting learning because they have an incomplete understanding of expectations, and accept SEN pupils' efforts too readily, without a sufficient level of challenge.
Inadequate (4)	• Teaching assistants are utilised inadequately due to poor management. • Teaching assistants lack the necessary knowledge, skills and understanding, thus contributing little to lessons, and SEN pupils' learning and well-being.

depressed and uncertain about moving on. These pupils worry about attending a much larger school; whether they will make friends; how they will cope with being taught by many different teachers; whether they will be able to do the work in class; whether they will be bullied by older pupils; and how they will travel to secondary school.

The role of SENCO in relation to transfer and transition

A SENCO will work in partnership with other staff who will take a lead on transfer in both schools, as well as liaising closely with the parents of SEN pupils. A Year 6 SENCO will discuss the provision for SEN pupils at secondary school in Year 7 with the high school SENCO, focusing on ensuring that the continuity in the Year 6 pupils' learning will be maintained.

SENCOs in both schools may also wish to explore:

• how they foresee the National Strategies *Progression Guidance* (DCSF, 2009f) being utilised on transfer, to raise staff expectations about SEN pupils' progress

• which intervention programmes have had the greatest impact on improving SEN pupils' outcomes in Year 6 and Year 7, and the opportunity to continue to follow through with the most effective interventions in the next phase of schooling

• which ECM pupil well-being outcomes SEN pupils need to continue to develop further.

Annual Survey of Teaching Assistant Support

Teacher: _____ Teaching Assistant: _____

Pupil: _____ Date: _____

Questions:

1. When is teaching assistant support most helpful and useful?

2. What is the best type of teaching assistant support from your point of view/for you?

    In-class support ☐   Work outside ☐   ICT support/ ☐   Other: (please specify)
                         the classroom   computer   _____
                                                                  _____

3. What allows teaching assistant support to be effective and work well?

4. Do you like being with the same teaching assistant/teacher all year?

    YES ☐   NO ☐

5. What has been the best and greatest teaching assistant achievement this year?

6. When is teaching assistant support least helpful, least effective or most challenging?

7. What would make teaching assistant support even better?

8. Any further comments on teaching assistant support you wish to make:

Thank you for completing this survey. Please return it to the SEN Coordinator.

Figure 3.3   Annual survey on teaching assistant support

Photocopiable:
Rita Cheminais' Handbook for New SENCOs © Rita Cheminais, 2010 (SAGE)

Additional support for SEN pupils prior to transfer

It is beneficial if SEN pupils have extra opportunities to discuss their anxieties about transfer in Circle Time, and in SEAL sessions in Year 6. Many secondary schools will enable Year 6 SEN pupils to have an extra taster day session in the summer term, prior to transfer. Some secondary schools may enable SEN pupils to visit and prepare for transfer earlier, in Year 5. Peer support transfer systems between some primary and secondary schools can enable Year 6 SEN pupils to text or blog a Year 7 'buddy', prior to transfer. Another example of good practice is utilising a transfer pupil passport, which enables the Year 6 pupil to identify their strengths, hobbies and interests, as well as their aspirations at secondary school. A further example of good practice, between a secondary and primary school to ensure the smooth transfer of a SEN pupil with more complex SEN, occured when the teaching assistant from Year 6 also transferred to Year 7 in September, to support a pupil in the first year of secondary schooling.

Points to remember

- Effective teaching for SEN pupils shares most of the characteristics of effective teaching for all pupils.
- SEN pupils in mainstream schools should make two levels of progress across a Key Stage.
- Qualitative and quantitative approaches should be utilised to identify SEN.
- Applications for examination access arrangements must be made in good time.
- SEN pupils should be offered a range of methods for reporting bullying.
- SEN pupils should ideally be involved in the recruitment and appointment of teaching assistants.
- The transfer of SEN pupils to secondary school could be considered earlier in Year 5.

 ### Further activities

The following questions, focused on aspects covered in this chapter, meet the requirements of the National Award for Special Educational Needs Coordination, and support reflection and professional development:

1. Which two barriers to learning and participation for pupils with SEN and/or disability present the greatest challenge in your school or setting? Describe how you will minimise and remove these barriers.

2. After analysing the summative SEN pupil-level attainment data, you notice there is a cohort of SEN pupils who have underachieved. Describe the action you would take to address the issue.

3. As SENCO, what evidence would you collect to demonstrate the impact teaching assistant support is having on improving SEN pupils' learning and progress?

4. Identify one issue relating to SEN pupil transfer or transition that requires improvement. Describe the actions you would take, working in partnership with other colleagues, to address the issue.

5. Which aspects of the SENCO coordination role do you consider you require further support and/or development in, and who can enable you to acquire the required knowledge, skills and understanding?

Downloadable materials

For downloadable materials for this chapter visit www.sagepub.co.uk/ritacheminais

Figure 3.2 Teaching Assistant job description

Figure 3.3 Annual Survey on teaching assistant support

Table 3.2 Good and outstanding progress for learners with SEN/LDD

4

Leading, developing and supporting colleagues in the workforce

> **This chapter covers the following TDA SENCO learning outcomes:**
>
> - **providing professional direction to the work of others: leading the SEN and Access Team**
> - **leading best practice in the teaching and learning of SEN pupils**
> - **enabling others to understand educational psychologists' reports**
> - **leadership and development of staff: coaching and mentoring**
> - **planning and delivering SEN INSET to build capacity in the workforce**
> - **supporting trainee and newly qualified teachers**
> - **undertaking small-scale action research on an aspect of SEN.**

Providing professional direction to the work of others: leading the SEN and Access team

An effective SEN and Access team, led by the SENCO in a school, helps to promote the inclusion of pupils with SEN and/or disabilities. A SENCO cannot implement SEN policy and provision alone, and therefore will be reliant on the support of others in this team, including those in the senior leadership team. Teamwork as a cooperative and collaborative process empowers others to develop professionally. Each member of the SEN and Access team will bring a range of knowledge, skills and expertise. The SENCO will maximise the team members' strengths, to help build capacity across the school among other colleagues.

Generally, within the team, particular members will take on specific roles, including the SENCO themselves. Belbin (1993) described the key roles that team members are likely to take on which are outlined below and would help to bring about the required changes in SEN policy and practice across the school:

- **Plant** – a highly creative individual who promotes new ideas and is good at solving problems.

- **Monitor-evaluator** – provides a critical eye, making impartial judgements and weighs up opinions in a dispassionate way.

- **Coordinator** – driven by the team objectives, encourages other team members and delegates work appropriately.

- **Resource investigator** – identifies and explores external ideas, providing the team with information and also ensures that the team's ideas are known externally.

- **Implementer** – turns ideas into practical, workable strategies which are as efficient as possible.

- **Completer-finisher** – 'polishes' and scrutinises work and ideas, acts as quality control.

- **Team worker** – is perceptive to other team members' feelings, needs and concerns, and helps them work together to complete the work required.

- **Shaper** – a challenging individual who drives the team forward without losing focus or momentum.

- **Specialist** – an individual with pre-existing SEN and inclusion skills and knowledge.

The SEN and Access team is likely to comprise of SEN teachers, higher-level teaching assistants, teaching assistants and learning mentors. Other external professionals will dip in and out of the team, according to the needs of children with SEN and/or disabilities. These may include: a school nurse, physiotherapist, occupational therapist, speech and language therapist, behaviour support teacher, educational psychologist, Connexions Personal Adviser, counsellor, social worker and educational welfare officer.

The core purpose of the SEN and Access team is to remove barriers to learning and participation for pupils with SEN and/or disabilities, in order to enable them to reach their optimum potential.

A SENCO would need to audit the skills of the SEN and Access team. The following checklist provides a valuable point of reference for them in identifying any aspects of teamwork which require further development.

Teamwork checklist

✓ All members of the team have a basic understanding of the principles of teamwork.

✓ All team members understand the decision-making process.

✓ The team as a whole is clear about its core purpose, expectations and collective responsibility for SEN pupils.

✓ All team members understand how their role fits into the bigger picture.

✓ There is a strong cohesive 'team spirit' based on mutual trust and respect.

✓ Core team members will have access to ongoing professional development.

✓ Every core team member will receive an annual appraisal.

✓ Team meetings will take place that are focused on developmental and operational activities.

✓ Team members will be able to use their initiative, be creative and share good practice.

✓ All team members will feel valued for the contributions they make.

✓ There will be a fair and equal distribution of work across the team.

✓ Team members' views will be listened to and respected.

Delegation and distributed leadership

Delegation is the process of entrusting somebody else with the appropriate responsibility for the accomplishment of a particular activity. Effective delegation means choosing the right tasks to delegate, identifying the right colleagues to delegate to, and delegating in a right and proper way.

Delegation of some operational tasks to members of the SEN and access team will enable a SENCO to spend more time on their strategic leadership role. Prior to delegating a task, they will need to answer the following questions:

• Is this a task that someone else in the SEN and Access team can do?

• Does the delegated task provide a real opportunity for that team member to develop professionally?

• Is the task likely to reoccur?

• Will I as SENCO have the time to advise, support and check on the progress of the person undertaking the delegated task?

• Have I identified the right person to undertake this task?

A SENCO should keep a log of the tasks they have delegated in order to ensure a fair distribution occurs across the team. This information can contribute evidence to individual team members' annual appraisal or performance management review.

Distributed leadership as a shared activity refers to the distribution of aspects of leadership across different staff at all levels, in order to divide up tasks and responsibilities more equitably. Distributed leadership is a group activity that works through and within relationships rather than individual action, and is dependent on who possesses the relevant expertise or creativity, irrespective of where they fail in the school staffing structure.

There are particular factors that can promote distributed leadership in a school. These are as follows:

• trust

• confidence

- a supportive, emotionally intelligent atmosphere

- a no-blame culture for risk taking where any mistake is viewed as a learning opportunity

- high-level communication

- openness and a willingness to change and to challenge

- a willingness to share and pursue common goals.

A couple of examples of distributed leadership in the SEN and Access team can been seen when a SENCO deploys teaching assistants to take on subject specialisms by attaching them to subject departments/teams as opposed to them being 'jack of all trades' and solely performing a generic in-class support role, and when teaching assistants with particular strengths and talents have led lunchtime or after-school clubs as part of the school's extended services' core offer.

The team members making up an SEN and Access team will need to record these types of distributed leadership activities in their portfolio of professional development.

Managing conflict and resistance to change

There may arise at some point in time conflicts of interests among team members within the SEN and Access team. It has to be recognised that conflict is an inevitable consequence of working with others and it does stop a team stagnating. In order to ensure these differences do not lead to a breakdown or disruption in working relationships, a SENCO will need to have an understanding of the basics of managing conflict and conflict resolution.

Conflict styles

Different conflict styles are useful in different situations, and a SENCO needs to be able to identify which style they should adopt when conflict arises. The five styles described below were first identified by Kenneth Thomas and Ralph Kilmann in the 1970s, and they are still relevant today:

- **Competitive** – using formal authority and a position of power, a firm stand is taken to make a fast decision, usually when an emergency arises.

- **Collaborative** – being assertive at the same time as being cooperative and understanding while acknowledging the concerns of others. This style is used for handling conflicts over very important issues, or to bring a variety of viewpoints together to get the best solution, or when there have been previous conflicts in the group.

- **Compromising** – trying to find a solution that will partially satisfy everyone. Everyone, including the compromiser, is expected to relinquish something. It is an appropriate style to use when dealing with moderately important issues.

- **Accommodating** – having a willingness to meet the needs of others at the expense of the person's own needs, i.e. being highly cooperative rather than assertive. This is a useful approach to adopt when the issue matters more to the other person, and when keeping the peace is more important than winning.

- **Avoiding** – evading conflict entirely, in order not to hurt anyone's feelings. It is a weak approach to take, and is often taken when the controversy is trivial, or someone else is in a better position to solve the problem (Thomas and Kilmann, 1974).

The conflict resolution strategy

This approach to resolving conflict will entail a SENCO following six key principles:

1. Ensure that good relationships are the first priority: build mutual respect, remain calm and constructive and be polite.

2. Separate the problem from the person: engage in a professional debate without damaging working relationships, and acknowledge that the other person is not really being 'difficult'.

3. Pay attention to the views or interests being presented: engage in active listening to better understand why the person feels that way, or holds that particular viewpoint.

4. Listen first, and then speak: listen to the other person to understand where they are coming from before defending your own or another's position.

5. Set out the facts: agree and establish the objective, observable elements that will impact on the decision.

6. Explore options jointly: be open and receptive to a 'third way' existing, enabling both parties to reach an amicable position.

Putting conflict resolution into practice

Adopting the following five-stepped approach, a SENCO will not only be able to resolve any conflict existing within the SEN and Access team, but also that existing between other staff in school, between parents and staff, and SEN pupils and staff.

Step 1: Set the scene

Begin by clarifying that the aim is to resolve the problem amicably through discussion, and summarise what the problem, issue or disagreement is about.

Step 2: Gather information

Listen to both viewpoints and clarify feelings in an attempt to understand the thinking, motivation and reasons behind each view. Establish whether the conflict is affecting the work performance of those involved, disrupting team work or impeding decision making, or affecting the delivery of additional provision to SEN pupils.

Step 3: Agree on the problem

Endeavour to reach a common perception of the problem or issue, or at least to understand what both parties see the problem as being.

Step 4: Brainstorm possible solutions

Engage both parties in generating possible solutions to the problem, and be open to suggestions and ideas.

Step 5: Negotiate a solution

Look for 'trade-offs', a common goal or compromise, and a win–win situation. Remain detached and impartial and be patient. Eventually, the conflict will be resolved at this final step.

Leading best practice in the teaching and learning of SEN pupils

A SENCO will very often be viewed by other colleagues in a school as being the 'expert' in SEN. Their role is to build capacity among the staff in the school, in order to stop this 'learned helplessness' and dependency model. The Primary and Secondary National Strategies have produced some excellent resources to support SENCOs in their strategic leadership role in embedding and implementing SEN policy and provision in the whole school.

The Primary National Strategy resource *Leading on Inclusion* (DfES, 2005a) focuses on three aspects: self-evaluation; understanding and using data; and planning effective provision. The Key Stage 3 National Strategy resource entitled *Maximising Progress: Ensuring the Attainment of Pupils with SEN* covers using data and target setting; approaches to learning and teaching; and managing the learning process (DfES, 2005c, d, e). The Secondary National Strategy resource entitled *Effective Leadership* (DfES, 2006a) covers using data to track and monitor pupils' progress; managing the deployment of additional adults; and reviewing other areas of school improvement in relation to the progress of pupils with SEN and/or disabilities. All these publications have further strengthened the SENCO's strategic role in ensuring SEN becomes everyone's responsibility across a school.

In order to lead best practice in SEN effectively across a school, the SENCO's key role will be to:

- model effective classroom practice for teaching pupils with SEN

- support teachers in identifying the barriers to learning and participation and to be aware of which teaching approaches and learning strategies to utilise

- advise on and support teacher planning to meet the needs of SEN pupils

- advise on behaviour management

- provide guidance on curriculum differentiation to enhance access

- advise on ICT software to support SEN pupils' learning

- provide guidance on target setting

- advise on engaging SEN pupils in reviewing their own progress

- advise on smaller stepped assessment, i.e. P levels

- advise on what constitutes good progress for SEN pupils

- provide guidance on the effective deployment of teaching assistants

- coach or mentor other teachers to meet the needs of SEN pupils

- disseminate the findings from research on good practice in teaching pupils with SEN

- signpost to further sources of support and information.

In leading best practice in SEN across the school, a SENCO should aim to:

- make a positive difference to SEN pupils' learning

- influence and make a significant contribution to the professional learning of other colleagues within the school

- build up and strengthen relationships of trust with colleagues

- establish a professional dialogue with other staff on meeting the needs of SEN pupils

- help develop greater confidence and competence among other staff in meeting a diversity of high-incidence special educational needs.

Enabling others to understand educational psychologists' reports

Newly appointed SENCOs will receive a copy of an educational psychologist's (EP) report for each child as part of the SEN statutory assessment process, and also for any subsequent annual statement reviews. These reports will contain technical jargon, which may not appear to be very user-friendly to parents and teachers. It is helpful if SENCOs can translate the technical terms contained in these reports into a more understandable language that will help parents, teaching and support staff to understand what the SEN child's needs, capabilities and barriers to learning and participation are, and how best to meet their needs. There are two excellent resources that SENCOs can refer to, which will help them to translate this technical professional jargon into simpler terms for others.

Table 4.1   Components of an educational psychologist's report

Section of the EP report	Features
1. Name of referrer	• Child's current learning situation • Child's general abilities
2. Nature of the child's difficulty	• Full description of the child's difficulties and problems in relation to learning and/or social, emotional, personal development and behaviour
3. Relevant history of the child	• Child's developmental history • Child's developmental milestones • Child's home and school background • Parental opinion of their child's progress in school • Teacher/SENCO comments
4. Assessment information	• The type of standardised diagnostic and/or screening assessment tests used by the EP, the most common being the British Ability Scales (BAS) and the Weschler Intelligence Scale for Children (WISC) • Details of how the child presented during assessment • Child's strengths and weaknesses, abilities, rates of progress and feelings • Findings from the EP's direct observations of the child in the school and classroom setting • Information from other professionals and school assessments
5. Conclusions and recommendations	• The EP's recommended strategies and approaches the school should adopt to help minimise the child's barriers to learning and participation • An outline of the educational provision required which includes: curriculum modifications and access arrangements; additional interventions or programmes; size and type of teaching group; additional adult support required to meet objectives • Goals and objectives for the child, the parents/carers and the school • Nature and frequency of planning, monitoring and evaluating the provision

The first resource is *Psychobabble: A Parents' Guide to Psychological Reports* by Stephanie Lorenz (1997), and the second publication is *Tribunal Toolkit*, available from the Advisory Centre for Education at www.ace-ed.org.uk (1997). The ACE resource exemplifies an actual EP report for a child and translates the technical jargon within it. It also provides a comprehensive glossary of the professional terminology EPs may use in their reports, and gives details about the types of diagnostic and screening assessment tools they are likely to utilise when undertaking a child's assessment. Table 4.1 provides an overview of the component parts of an EP's report. Educational psychologists in their reports will refer to percentile ranks to express a child's intelligence. These may appear to be very technical to a parent or teacher unfamiliar with this indicator, and SENCOs may value using the following example to explain what a percentile rank means.

Explanation of percentile rank

If a child's EP report indicated that they were in the 87th percentile, this would mean that out of a group of 100 children of the same age, that child is in the top 13%, and 87 children were not as capable as the child.

Alternatively:

If a child's EP report indicated that they were in the 5th percentile, this would mean that out of a group of 100 children of the same age, 95 children scored better than the child who has been assessed.

The national standardised score in the SATs results is an indicator of a child's potential and a SENCO may prefer to signpost teachers and support staff to this measure. An SEN pupil who has a standardised score of 70–75 is considered to have moderate learning difficulties. An average pupil has a standardised score of 100. Reading age and spelling age for an SEN pupil will be the most helpful assessment information that SENCOs would wish to share with teachers, in order to ensure they personalise the curriculum at the appropriate level to match the child's level of functioning. Chapter 3 in this book provides further information about these assessments tests, in the section on examination concessions for SEN pupils.

Leadership and development of staff: coaching and mentoring

A SENCO may take on either role within their own school, and where they do so, they must have sufficient quality time to commit to the role:

- **Coaching** is a structured sustained process for enabling the development of a specific aspect of a professional learner's (coachee) practice. It doesn't tell the coachee what to do, but instead helps them to find their own solutions to a particular problem.

- **Mentoring** is a process for supporting teachers, as professional learners, through significant career transitions.

Ten principles to effective coaching and mentoring

1. Using structured professional dialogue which is evidence-based from practice.

2. Establishing the ground rules and boundaries of the coaching/mentoring relationship.

3. Coachee/mentee taking increasing responsibility for their own professional development throughout the process.

4. Understanding the theory and how it works in practice in various contexts.

5. Trying out new approaches in practice in a learning environment that supports risk taking and innovation.

6. Building up trust, mutual respect and sensitivity between the coach/mentor and the coachee/mentee.

7. Procuring specialist expertise to extend the skills and knowledge of the coachee/mentee, and to model good practice.

8. Identifying and setting coachee/mentee agreed personal goals.

9. Recognising the benefits of the experience for coaches and mentors.

10. Sustaining regular professional learning, action and reflection on behalf of the coachee/mentee.

SENCOs may find it helpful to refer to the DfES National Framework for Mentoring and Coaching, which is included in the Primary National Strategy resource *Leading on Intervention* (DfES, 2006b).

Types and styles of coaching

- **Informal coaching conversations** – happen when a school leader or leading teacher utilises coaching principles during short informal conversations about an issue raised by a colleague. It models a professional learning dialogue and supports the development of reflective thinking and practice.

- **Specialist coaching** – this utilises specialist knowledge with a coachee to develop their practice in a specific area, e.g. SEN, or in a subject specialism or pedagogy. The coach will also have effective practice in coaching skills, qualities and principles.

- **Collaborative peer co-coaching** – involves partner teachers providing non-judgemental support to each other based on evidence from their own practice. Co-coaches each take on the role of coach and professional learner.

- **Team coaching** – is usually led by an external specialist coach or an internally experienced coach, and is focused on improvement in pedagogy, a particular subject/aspect, e.g. SEN, or a phase (primary or secondary).

- **Expert coaching** – entails an expert external coach or a leading teacher working to develop coaching skills across the school.

- **Self-coaching** – involves coaching principles and protocols being utilised by an individual on issues of professional concern to them.

- **Pupil coaching** – covers the promotion of pupil-to-pupil coaching, led by skilled teacher-coaches within a school.

SENCOs are most likely to be engaged in informal coaching conversations and specialist coaching with colleagues focused on meeting the needs of SEN pupils.

Key skills for SENCOs as coaches

Ten essential key skills that SENCOs as coaches will require include the ability to:

- **relate sensitively** to the coachee to build up trust and confidence

- **model expertise** in practice through professional dialogue

- **facilitate access to research and evidence** to support the development of the coachee's pedagogic practice

- **tailor activities** in partnership and agreement with the coachee

- **observe, analyse and reflect** on the coachee's practice and make this explicit, giving them the chance to share their perceptions

- **provide information** that enables learning from mistakes and success

- **facilitate a growing independence** in professional learning

- **use open questions** which are clear, concise, neutral, purposeful and non-judgemental. The questions asked by a SENCO as coach will raise awareness, explore beliefs, and help the coachee to understand the problems and develop their own solutions. (The Primary National Strategy resource *Leading on Intervention* (DfES, 2006b) provides an excellent bank of suggested questions for coaches to utilise.)

- **listen actively**, building in periods of silence to develop thinking and suggestions from the coachee

- **establish buffer zones** between coaching and other formal relationships with the coachee in school.

Figure 4.1 illustrates the four main stages to coaching, while Figure 4.2 provides a model template for the SENCO as coach to record the coaching activity. This would be used in agreement with the coachee.

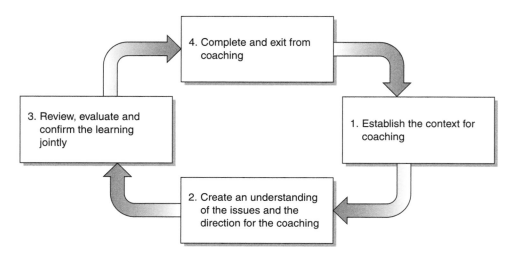

Figure 4.1 Four stages to coaching

Name of coachee: _____
Name of coach: _____
Date of coaching session: _____

Focus 1:

Information recorded	Comments, observations and questions for feedback

Focus 2:

Information recorded	Comments, observations and questions for feedback

Focus 3:

Information recorded	Comments, observations and questions for feedback

Figure 4.2   Recording sheet for a coaching session

 Photocopiable:

The GROW model of coaching

The GROW model of coaching is an effective popular coaching model which is an approach recommended by the National College for Leadership of Schools and Children's Services, as well as by the TDA. The acronym G-R-O-W represents the stages of a coaching conversation/session:

G = Goal; **R** = Reality; **O** = Options; **W** = Will

SENCOs may find this coaching model appropriate to utilise with any SEN and Access team member who is new to the role, or facing an issue with an aspect of their work.

Table 4.2 illustrates the stages in the GROW model of coaching.

SENCOs as mentors

A SENCO is most likely to act as a mentor for the induction of a newly qualified teacher or a new member of staff joining their team or department who is also new to the school. A mentoring partnership can be a very rewarding, enriching experience in terms of helping others to develop professionally and become more effective in their job. Mentoring, like coaching, will bring an added time commitment for a SENCO, who must be certain beforehand that they will be able to protect this allocated time in order to carry out this important role.

What mentoring involves

Mentoring will involve a SENCO as a mentor in the following activities:

- identifying learning goals and supporting the teacher's progression

- developing and increasing the mentee's control over their learning

- active listening

- modelling good practice in the inclusion of SEN pupils, observing the mentee teaching, articulating and discussing practice to raise awareness

- engaging in shared learning experiences, e.g. team teaching, lesson observation, or watching Teachers TV video recordings of lessons

- providing guidance, feedback and direction to the mentee

- reviewing the mentee's progress and supporting action planning

- contributing to the assessment and appraisal of the mentee

- brokering access to further professional development opportunities, e.g. visiting other schools, including a special school.

A SENCO may find it useful to ask the mentee at the end of the year to reflect on the following questions:

Table 4.2 GROW steps to structure a coaching session

GROW Stage	Action	Coach's question prompts for coachee
Establish the **Goal**	1. Agree the goal or outcome to be achieved 2. Establish a clear picture of success and be positive	• How will you know you have achieved the goal? • How will you know the problem is solved?
Examine the **Reality**	1. The team member/coachee describes their current reality 2. An honest appraisal of the situation is made 3. An understanding of what has already been achieved is clarified	• What is happening now? • What, who, when, how often? • What is the effect or result of that?
Explore the **Options**	1. Exploration of what is possible, i.e. all the possible options available for solving the problem are generated by the team member/coachee with the help of the coach 2. Assumptions are challenged 3. There are opportunities to be creative in exploring the options	• What else can you do? • What if this or that constraint were removed? • What are the benefits, advantages or disadvantages of each option? • What factors will you consider to weigh up the options?
Establish the **Will**	1. Get the team member/coachee to commit to a specific action, and establish the next steps and actions 2. Gain a commitment to change, and identify any support needed for the coachee/team member 3. Ensure any obstacles are understood and tackled	• What will you do and when? • What could stop you moving forward and how will you overcome that issue? • Will this address your goal? • How likely is this option to succeed? • What else will you do?

1. How do you feel the year has gone in relation to teaching pupils with SEN?

2. What do you consider have been your most significant achievements in SEN this year?

3. Which, if any, aspects of your work teaching SEN pupils have you found most challenging?

4. Which aspects of your work with SEN pupils would you wish to develop further?

Planning and delivering SEN INSET to build capacity in the workforce

Schools' continuing professional development (CPD) budgets are not extensive and therefore the most cost-effective training option is likely to be SENCOs delivering INSET sessions in-house. Delivering INSET to colleagues within your own school can either be daunting if you are new to the SENCO role, or 'comfortable' and non-threatening because of knowing the audience.

A SENCO may wish to review the other options available as to who would be best to deliver the INSET and/or share the input with them. A SENCO may also consider asking a suitably experienced SENCO from another school, or professionals from the local authority such as the Educational Psychologist, the SEN Adviser or SEN and Inclusion Consultant, or other practitioners from Children's Services, depending on the aspect of SEN being covered. If the budget permits, a SENCO may choose to commission a national guest speaker.

Once they know who will be leading the training session on SEN, a SENCO will need to begin to prepare for the session, usually one or two weeks before the event. The session should be comprised of direct input and a range of practical tasks, which will require colleagues to think, discuss, analyse, plan and undertake a follow-up activity back in the classroom.

Tips for planning and preparing the content of the SEN INSET

1. Define the scope and content of the INSET session. Plan the session using a concept map/mind map to record ideas, concepts and key content, and number each aspect on the mind map in order of priority. Identify where the practical tasks will fit in.

2. Consider the specific needs of the audience – what do they already know about the topic? Content must be relevant and practical and enable the staff to benefit from acquiring new knowledge, as well as to learn strategies they can apply and try out in their classroom.

3. Organise the direct presentation using the following structure:

   a five-minute opener, e.g. a story/anecdote, a real scenario, facts, a quiz; followed by three chunks of seven minutes each, focused on three different key aspects of the SEN topic, using some variety to deliver the message, e.g. pictures, cartoons, sound, animation; finishing with a 'closer' of four minutes to allow time for questions, giving out handouts and ending with a memorable 'big' finish with a call for action.

4. Produce the PowerPoint slides transferring the ideas and information from the mind map. Don't have too many slides (i.e. one slide per minute). Use a font size of between 20 to 30 and Arial for the font type. Keep the slides simple – use three or four short sentences or bullet points per slide. Check spelling and grammar, and avoid an overuse of jargon and acronyms. Give subtle backgrounds to slides. Use humour selectively in the presentation.

5. Practise the presentation to check the time it takes to deliver this. Check that the version your presentation is in will be compatible with the computer you will be using at the session – if not, use your own laptop computer.

6. On the day of the INSET, open the presentation by informing the audience of how long you intend to speak for, and what the programme for the session will be comprised of. Don't read out each slide word for word. Make eye contact with the audience. Seek audience participation. Split the presentation into segments, with practical tasks followed by reflection on a PowerPoint slide.

7. Limit the number of questions you take after the presentation from the audience to two or three, and ask colleagues to leave any further questions on 'Post-it' notes for you to respond to later on in the week.

Figure 4.3 provides an example of a SENCO's PowerPoint presentation for a twilight INSET on SEN pupil voice.

Supporting trainee and newly qualified teachers

A SENCO plays a crucial role in providing advice, guidance and support to trainee and newly qualified teachers (NQTs) on SEN, disability and inclusive classroom practice. A SENCO may wish to give trainees and NQTs an SEN CPD audit to identify which aspects of SEN they require further information and support with.

Figure 4.4 provides an example of a model SEN CPD audit which a SENCO can tailor and customise accordingly.

Some SENCOs will offer a weekly or fortnightly lunchtime drop-in session for staff, which NQTs can attend, where they can bring any concerns, queries or issues relating to SEN.

OFSTED, in its report entitled *How Well New Teachers are Prepared to Teach Pupils with Learning Difficulties and/or Disabilities*, which was published in September 2008 (OFSTED, 2008a), identified that of the schools surveyed, few gave newly qualified teachers (NQTs) enough coverage of learning difficulties (LDD) in their induction programme. Similarly, in relation to initial teacher education (ITE), there were considerable variations in practice, coverage and the quality of training in LDD.

LISTENING TO THE SEN PUPIL VOICE

Spring Term 2011
Leafy Lane School
Presented by the SENCO

SYNOPSIS OF SESSION

- What does good listening entail? Top ten tips
- Why should adults listen to a pupil voice?
- Which pupils must be listened to?
- What are national surveys telling us?
- Practical pupil voice activities to promote good listening
- Signposting to further information

WHAT DO WE MEAN BY LISTENING?

- Paying attention to what the pupil has to say
- Having an open mind and attitude
- Respecting and empathising with pupils' feelings
- Empowering pupils to participate meaningfully in decisions that affect their lives
- Tuning in to the pupil agenda
- Acting in response to what a pupil has said

WHAT DOES GOOD LISTENING ENTAIL?

- A readiness to wait for a pupil to speak
- The ability to tolerate periods of silence
- The ability to avoid making interruptions when a pupil is speaking
- Observing a pupil's moods, gestures and body language

(Continued)

Figure 4.3 Example of a SENCO PowerPoint presentation

 **Photocopiable:**

Rita Cheminais' Handbook for New SENCOs © Rita Cheminais, 2010 (SAGE)

Figure 4.3 *(Continued)*

WHY SHOULD ADULTS LISTEN TO PUPILS?

o **Legal requirements** – Children Acts 1989 and 2004
   Have regard to the ascertainable wishes and feelings of the child

o **Human rights** – UNCRC Article 12
   To the child who is capable of forming his or her own views the right to express those views in all matters affecting the child, the view of the child being given due weight in accordance with the age and maturity of the child

o **Moral reasons** – Every Child Matters provides the moral purpose for listening to pupils' views and opinions, in order to ensure better outcomes

o **More effective children's workforce practitioners** – who have the skills and knowledge to listen to and respect pupils' views, and therefore provide more appropriate interventions

WHAT ARE CHILDREN AND YOUNG PEOPLE TELLING ADULTS ABOUT THEIR WELL-BEING NATIONALLY?

The Good Childhood Inquiry 2007–2008 found:

o 29% of young people long for someone to turn to for advice
o 49% of children feel under a lot of pressure at school

OFSTED TellUs Survey found the biggest worries of pupils are:

o 51% exams; 39% friendships; 35% school work; 32% being healthy; 30% their future

4Children My Shout Out Survey 2007 found:

o 78% of children worry about bullying

PIRLS Survey 2006 found:

o Only 30% of 10-year-olds feel safe in the classroom

(Continued)

TOP TEN TIPS FOR LISTENING TO PUPIL VOICE

1. Stop, look and listen
2. Keep an open mind to what is said
3. Give the pupil some control
4. Start from where the pupil is
5. Give permission to talk
6. Avoid direct questions
7. Offer prompts and triggers
8. Provide information and explanations
9. Encourage questions
10. Check for understanding

HOW MANY PUPILS WILL HAVE ADDITIONAL NEEDS IN A SCHOOL AND NEED TO BE LISTENED TO?

In an average secondary school of 1000 pupils, according to Young Minds:

o 100 pupils will have self-harmed by the age of 16
o 100 pupils will be suffering from mental health problems and experiencing significant distress
o 50 pupils will be seriously depressed
o 20 pupils will have obsessive compulsive disorder (OCD)
o 10 pupils will have an eating disorder
o 5–10 pupils will have attempted suicide

In a class of 20 pupils:

o two will have a clinically defined mental health problem
o another two may experience psychological problems that require specialist help

Figure 4.3 *(Continued)*

SEN PUPIL VOICE POSTCARD ACTIVITY

**What I like best about
my extra help in school**

**What more could be
done to help me**

TALKING PICTURES ACTIVITY

○ The pupil is asked to use photographs, pictures or
drawings to form a table mat to show their thoughts
and ideas in response to the statements below:

○ *'Where I could go on my magic carpet?'*

Or,

○ *'Look through the keyhole to see my biggest secret'.*

MY IMPORTANT THINGS

The pupil writes their favourite thing or person in each square.
The adult will then listen to the pupil as they explain each of these.

1	2	3
4	5	6

FOCUSED DISCUSSION: LISTENING
TO SEN PUPIL VIEWS

○ Can you tell me why you feel happy today?

○ How are things going for you in school?

○ What has been your best achievement this term?

○ What have you found hard to do in school?

○ Who could help you more with school work?

(Continued)

Figure 4.3 *(Continued)*

SMALL GROUP ACTIVITY ON SEN PUPIL VOICE

- What five things could the head teacher do to make things better for you in school?

- How could you help the head teacher to do these things?

WORDS OF WISDOM

'The reason why we have two ears and only one mouth is that we may listen the more and speak the less.'

(Greek Philosopher Zeno of Citium 333–246 BC)

REFLECTION

- What have been your thoughts about what you heard today?

- What will be the first idea you will use from today's session with the pupils?

USEFUL RESOURCES AND REFERENCES

www.goodchild.org.uk

www.havingavoice.org

DCSF (2008) *Working Together: Listening to the Voices of Children and Young People*

Alison McLeod (2008) *Listening to Children: A Practitioner's Guide* (Jessica Kingsley)

Rita Cheminais (2008) *Engaging Pupil Voice to Ensure that Every Child Matters* (Routledge)

SEN Staff Training Audit

Name: _____ Role: _____

From the list of topics below, please choose three and number in order of priority.

- ☑ **Identifying special educational needs (SEN)**

- ☑ **Managing pupils' emotional and behavioural difficulties**

- ☑ **Meeting the needs of pupils with specific learning difficulties**

- ☑ **Meeting the needs of pupils with speech, language and communication needs**

- ☑ **Meeting the needs of pupils with dual and/or multiple exceptionalities**

- ☑ **Differentiating the curriculum**

- ☑ **Removing barriers to learning and participation**

- ☑ **Assessment for learning and pupils with SEN**

- ☑ **Using the P levels**

- ☑ **Data analysis and using the Progression Guidance for SEN pupils**

- ☑ **Target setting for pupils with SEN**

- ☑ **Working in partnership with the parents and carers of SEN pupils**

- ☑ **Making best use of ICT to enhance SEN pupils' access to learning**

- ☑ **Making best use of teaching assistants to support SEN pupils' learning**

- ☑ **Meeting the OFSTED inspection requirements for SEN and disability**

- ☑ **Meeting the requirements of the disability legislation**

- ☑ **Developing SEN pupil 'voice' to review their own progress and provision**

- ☑ **Any other SEN topic** (Please specify: _____)

Please indicate your preferred method for accessing the training selected:

External course	☐	**Online/CD/DVD**	☐
SENCO drop-in	☐	**Virtual learning platform**	☐
Printed information	☐	**e-forum/e-conferencing**	☐
School INSET	☐	**Workshops in-house**	☐

Figure 4.4   SEN training audit for NQTs and other staff

Photocopiable:

Rita Cheminais' Handbook for New SENCOs © Rita Cheminais, 2010 (SAGE)

OFSTED, in the same report, went on to identify best practice for NQTs, in enabling them to meet the needs of pupils with LDD. SENCOs may find it useful to download this report from the OFSTED website at www.ofsted.gov.uk and then use it to plan and inform NQT professional development sessions in SEN.

In 2009, the TDA, via the TTRB website, launched initial teacher training materials on SEN/LDD for primary and secondary undergraduates with an accompanying toolkit. The materials can be downloaded from www.ttrb.ac.uk. Similarly, the General Teaching Council for England (GTC) has an excellent online resource entitled *Making SENse of CPD,* which can be accessed at www.gtce.org.uk/networks/sen/

SENCOs would be well advised to familiarise themselves with these two resources, prior to supporting NQTs on their induction, in order to use and refer to relevant modules from them and provide support for their practice. In addition, the SENCO will signpost NQTs to the National Strategies' Inclusion Development Programme (IDP) resources, which can be accessed online at www.standards dcsf.gov.uk/nation alstrategies/inclusion/sen/idp

The role of SENCOs in supporting trainee and newly qualified teachers

SENCOs' input with trainee and NQTs should ideally cover:

- clarifying the SENCO role and the SEN governor role

- familiarising them with the school's SEN policy and SEN systems

- explaining the range of additional and different provision for SEN pupils

- advising on the identification of SEN and what type of evidence to collect

- providing a guide to SEN acronyms and key terminology

- providing advice on target setting and IEPs (where they are being used)

- arranging visits to other local schools and resourced provisions

- arranging a session on the role of various external agencies

- understanding and meeting the emotional, social and behavioural needs of pupils

- assessing SEN pupils' progress and attainment

- using the P levels and the National Strategies' *Progression Guidance*

- advising on the effective deployment of teaching assistants

- providing advice on quality first teaching, personalised learning and curriculum differentiation

- providing advice on making reasonable adjustments for pupils with disabilities

- advising on working in partnership with parents/carers of SEN pupils.

Undertaking small-scale research focused on effective practice for SEN

A SENCO, as a teacher-researcher, is an active change agent and innovator who aims, through action research, to identify any gaps in practice in order to make things better and improve the 'status quo' within their own school in an aspect of SEN and/or disability policy and provision.

Action research entails investigating an idea, issue or problem relating to current SEN practice, which in turn requires further explanation in order to reach a conclusion or solution based on the evidence gathered.

Dr Christine Macintyre (2000) offers some basic principles and rules in relation to the action research process. These are important for those who are undertaking research in settings in terms of targeting, managing and sharing research.

A SENCO would be advised to:

1. Choose an aspect of SEN that is relevant and important to them in the context of where they work which will extend the understanding of other colleagues as well as themselves.

2. Check that there is sufficient recent literature in existence on the SEN topic to provide guidance and a direction to the research.

3. Formulate a clear and concise research question or hypothesis on what exactly they, as the SENCO, want to find out.

4. Plan a series of manageable actions which use appropriate research methods to investigate the question or hypothesis.

5. Analyse the evidence and findings from the research undertaken to reach an overall conclusion, and make recommendations for the next steps leading to improvement.

Figure 4.5 illustrates the action research process.

Ideally, a SENCO's action research should show a development of influence or a new understanding and/or an improvement in practice in relation to SEN. Change as an outcome of action research will take time and SENCOs must not expect to change everything at once in their school in relation to SEN. However, they can lead by example, by changing an aspect of their own practice, which will help other colleagues to learn from their research experience. A SENCO will need to pilot some research methods initially, particularly if they are new to using them.

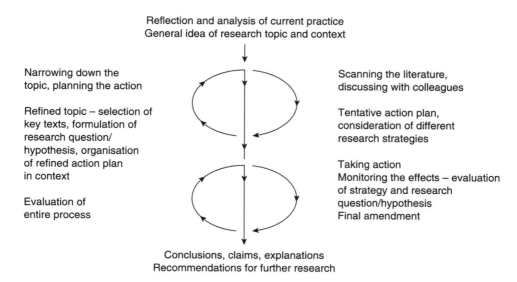

Reflection and analysis of current practice
General idea of research topic and context

Narrowing down the
topic, planning the action

Refined topic – selection of
key texts, formulation of
research question/
hypothesis, organisation
of refined action plan
in context

Evaluation of
entire process

Scanning the literature,
discussing with colleagues

Tentative action plan,
consideration of different
research strategies

Taking action
Monitoring the effects – evaluation
of strategy and research
question/hypothesis
Final amendment

Conclusions, claims, explanations
Recommendations for further research

Figure 4.5   The action research cycle

Source: Koshy, 2009

It is useful for SENCOs to have a 'critical friend' who can act as a sounding board, to share thoughts and action research findings with, and who can also offer impartial advice and guidance. This may be a senior colleague within the school, or a skilled and experienced SENCO from another school, or a professional from the local authority or a higher education institution. In addition, other staff, parents and pupils can be involved in school-based research relating to SEN and/or disability, as they can offer valuable insights which can then help to inform improvements in SEN policy and provision.

The benefits of undertaking small-scale action research

The benefits of undertaking small-scale action research are as follows:

- A SENCO has the autonomy to decide what to investigate.

- Action research enables a SENCO to check their perceptions of what is happening against that of others in the school, in relation to SEN.

- Action research can help a SENCO and others to have a better understanding about an aspect of SEN.

- A developed understanding about SEN helps a SENCO and others to evaluate their practice and change it as necessary.

- A SENCO's new and improved way of working can influence others to change.

- The school becomes a learning community of 'enquirers' who can share their learning and experience in SEN.

Suggestions for possible action research questions for SENCOs

1. There are too many pupils being identified in the school at the Action stage on the SEN Code of Practice who are not truly SEN.

2. Expectations among staff in school are too low in relation to SEN pupils' progress.

3. Inclusion isn't working in this school because the number of SEN pupils who are persistent absentees or excluded has risen in the last 12 months.

4. The additional literacy interventions used in school with SEN pupils are demonstrating little impact and poor added value.

5. SEN pupils in a year group are not achieving good enough ECM well-being outcomes compared to their peers.

6. The current deployment of teaching assistants in school is not making a significant difference to the achievement and attainment of SEN pupils.

7. Pupils with dual or multiple exceptionalities don't appear to be included on the school's gifted and talented register.

8. The staff in school perceive personalised learning as making little if any difference to SEN pupils' attainment and progress.

9. The contextualised value added for SEN pupils in this school is not good enough.

10. Measuring the impact of multi-agency interventions and extended service provision on SEN pupils' learning and well-being outcomes is complex.

11. The emphasis on Every Child Matters is reducing the staff commitment to identifying and meeting the needs of SEN pupils.

Figure 4.6 provides a template for an action research project.

Points to remember

- Teamwork and delegation will enhance the SENCO strategic role.
- Coaching and mentoring will help to develop staff confidence in SEN.
- Simplifying jargon will enable staff and parents to understand EP reports.
- SENCO support for trainee and NQTs should be ongoing.
- The aim should be to use one PowerPoint slide per minute with a maximum of three or four short points per slide.
- Action research helps SENCOs to effect change based on evidence.

Name:	School/Setting:

Project title/hypothesis:

Introduction and rationale:

Research project aims:

Research methodology:

Research findings:

Key recommendations:

Conclusion:

Figure 4.6   Template for a small-scale action research project

Photocopiable:

Further activities

The following questions, focused on aspects covered in this chapter, meet the requirements of the National Award for Special Educational Needs Coordination, and support reflection and professional development:

1. A teaching assistant reports that a staff member is struggling to teach his/her class which has a large number of SEN pupils in it. As SENCO, describe how you would tackle this issue.

2. An NQT in school requests a change of teaching assistant due to a conflict of interests existing between both parties, but the teaching assistant is effective in supporting a complex SEN pupil in the NQT's class. Outline the action you would take to resolve this situation.

3. Describe how you would evaluate the impact of any SEN INSET you have delivered in school.

4. Some school staff indicate that they haven't got the time to work through the Inclusion Development Programme resources. Describe the action you would take to address this issue.

Downloadable materials

For downloadable materials for this chapter visit www.sagepub.co.uk/ritacheminais

Figure 4.2 Recording sheet for a coaching session

Figure 4.3 Example of a SENCO PowerPoint presentation

Figure 4.4 SEN training audit for NQTs and other staff

Figure 4.6 Template for a small-scale action research project

5

Working in partnership with pupils, families and other professionals

This chapter covers the following TDA SENCO learning outcomes:

- consulting, engaging and communicating with colleagues, parents/carers and pupils in:

  - valuing the role and contributions of parents and carers of pupils with SEN and/or disabilities
  - communicating effectively with parents and carers
  - engaging pupil voice

- drawing on external sources of support and expertise:

  - the role of multi-agency professionals working with SEN pupils
  - developing and evaluating multi-agency partnerships

- utilising other external systems of support including:

  - the Children's Trust
  - the National Service Framework (NSF)
  - ContactPoint
  - the Common Assessment Framework (CAF) process
  - the lead professional
  - the team around the child (TAC).

Consulting, engaging and communicating with colleagues, parents/carers and pupils to enhance pupils' learning and achievement

Valuing the role and contributions of parents and carers of pupils with SEN and/or disabilities

The government, in the publication *Every Parent Matters*, states:

> Parents are usually the best judges of what children need. They understand their children better than anyone else, and have important insights into what children want. (DfES, 2007a: 6)

Eighty-seven per cent of a child's time during a school year is spent at home with their parents. The parents of children with SEN and/or disabilities, in particular, will have valuable knowledge and a good insight about their child's capabilities, achievements and needs that they could share with the SENCO at school.

The children of parents who take an active interest in their education tend to make greater progress in their learning. Family influences have been found to have a more powerful effect on children's achievements than either school or neighbourhood factors. Parents/carers are essential partners in their child's education, especially in view of the fact that they are the primary educators of their child. Parents are 'experts' on their own child, and a SENCO needs to respect and value their views and opinions and draw upon their knowledge and experience.

The parents/carers of children with SEN and/or disabilities will want to be reassured that the school and its staff will:

- accept and value their child for their uniqueness and difference

- focus on their child's strengths and 'hidden' talents

- understand the needs of the child's family and seek support for them during times of stress and increased pressure

- understand fully the child's special educational needs and/or disabilities, medical needs or special dietary needs

- offer the appropriate facilities and care for the SEN child, when they are feeling unwell or require medication to be administered

- be tolerant, sensitive and positive about the child's SEN.

The SEN Code of Practice (DfES, 2001b) offers some useful guidance to SENCOs about working in partnership with the parents/carers of pupils with SEN and/or disabilities (See Chapter 2, para 2.7).

Communicating effectively with parents and carers of pupils with SEN and/or disabilities

Schools have a duty to take account of the views of parents/carers and to listen to what they have to say, especially as they have relevant first-hand experience and informa-tion to share about their child. The majority of parents and carers will genuinely want to do the best for their child and will desire to work in partnership with the school. They will also be willing to cooperate when they can see and understand the real ben-efits of doing so in terms of helping to support their child's learning and well-being.

Regular communication with the parents/carers of pupils with SEN and/or disabili-ties is crucial in order to keep them up to date with their child's achievements, any changes in SEN provision, or the child's learning and well-being needs. It is always important for a SENCO to communicate in a way that suits the family situation and their preferences. Some SENCOs will offer a weekly telephone helpline or SEN 'drop-in' session for the parents/carers of pupils with SEN and/or disabilities.

The Lamb Inquiry on special educational needs and parental confidence (DCSF, 2009j) enabled the government to give parents greater rights and more of a say about their child's statement of SEN and the quality of their SEN provision. Indeed 2010 saw the introduction of a new national SEN helpline, providing independent expert advice and information directly to the parents of children with SEN and/or disabilities. A SENCO would also wish to seek the collective views of parents/carers about the school's SEN policy and provision. They may do this by issuing an annual parental questionnaire or survey, or alternatively by establishing a focus group of parent representatives of pupils with SEN and/or disabilities, who could maintain an ongoing two-way dialogue about SEN and disability developments in the school.

SENCOs should:

- respond promptly to any parental enquiries

- use plain non-technical language, avoiding acronyms when discussing a child's progress and SEN provision

- be honest but diplomatic in explaining to parents/carers the difficulties or problems a chid is experiencing in school

- give parents/carers an opportunity to say how they think a child could be helped more

- suggest practical strategies that parents/carers could use at home with a child, which will then complement what the school is doing

- actively listen to parents/carers

- seek clarification from parents/carers if uncertain about something they have said

- record parent/carer comments in writing, noting down the agreed next steps and actions to engage their involvement.

A SENCO needs to be able to ensure that they have secure evidence to feed into the school's self-evaluation form (SEF), which clearly demonstrates:

- the satisfaction levels of parents/carers of pupils with SEN and/or disabilities in relation to a child's provision in school

- the effectiveness of SENCO liaison and partnership working with parents and carers

- the impact and outcomes of parent partnership and liaison in informing any improvements or developments in school SEN policy and provision

- that they have acted upon the views of parents/carers of pupils with SEN and/or disabilities

- how they have engaged the 'hard to reach' parents/carers of these pupils

- the effectiveness of home–school communication with the parents/carers of pupils with SEN and/or disabilities.

SENCOs need to signpost parents/carers to other sources of useful information, i.e. the local Parent Partnership Service, the Family Support Worker, or the Parent Support Worker, where appropriate.

The DCSF produced a booklet for parents on SEN entitled *Special Educational Needs (SEN): A Guide for Parents and Carers* (2009b). A SENCO could produce a more parent-friendly leaflet from this DCSF guide as it is very lengthy and detailed. There is also a very good website called the Parents Centre, dedicated to SEN and disability, which is packed with information in a more parent-friendly format: www.parentscentre. gov.uk/educationandlearning/specialneeds/

Engaging pupil 'voice'

Engaging the 'voice' and participation of pupils with SEN and/or disabilities is integral to improving outcomes for these children and young people who, like all pupils, have a right to be consulted and to have their views taken seriously when decisions about them and their SEN provision are being made. If these pupils don't have an opportunity to have a say about their additional provision then they will only receive what adults think they need, which may not be appropriate. These pupils can recognise better than anyone the kinds of teaching and learning styles that are most helpful in enabling them to access the curriculum.

Articles 12 and 13 of the United Nations Convention on the Rights of the Child (UNCRC) 1989 give every child the right to express their views freely in all matters that affect them and to have the right to freedom of expression, i.e. the freedom to seek, receive and impart information and ideas of all kinds, either orally, in writing or in print, in the form of art, or through any other media of the child's choice.

Circle Time, a video diary room, blogging or text messaging, email and safe and secure chat rooms/forums offer alternative methods for capturing pupil voice. Not all pupils may be able or indeed willing to give their views to an adult. Others may not express their ideas, views or opinions in acceptable ways. The following is a list of suggested approaches which can enable pupils with more complex SEN to participate:

- voting cards/buttons

- drawings

- mind maps

- talking mats

- symbols

- 0–10 rating scales

- Post-it notes for a suggestion box.

Pupil 'voice' is beneficial in enabling a SENCO and other staff to gain a better understanding of what helps or hinders a learner's access or otherwise to learning, the curriculum and information. It can also help a SENCO to identify the strengths, weaknesses and any gaps in a school's SEN provision. They can share the following checklist with staff to promote SEN pupil 'voice':

☑ Put the pupil at ease prior to commencing discussion.

☑ Reassure the pupil that their views will be anonymous and confidential.

☑ Inform the pupil about the reasons for seeking their views.

☑ Avoid asking the pupil any leading questions.

☑ Phrase questions clearly.

☑ Actively listen to what the pupil says.

☑ Give pupils enough time to elaborate on their views and opinions.

☑ Whatever the pupil says, remain impartial and unbiased.

☑ Ask the pupil to justify/explain the views they have expressed.

☑ Check your understanding of the pupil's response by repeating it, e.g. 'When you said that … you meant …'.

☑ Let the pupil know which of the views will be acted upon and taken further.

☑ Let the pupil know which of their views cannot be acted upon immediately.

☑ Thank the pupil for their contribution and for sharing their views with you.

Finally, a SENCO would need to gather evidence for the school SEF to indicate:

• the ways in which they have gathered SEN pupils' views about their additional provision, their progress and achievements

• the frequency in gathering such views

• what the views of pupils with SEN and/or disabilities are indicating

• how these pupils' views are fed back to the relevant stakeholders

• any snapshots, cameos, brief case studies of the impact, outcome and changes occurring as a result of listening to SEN pupil voice.

Pupil-centred reviews are examples of good practice where the SEN child has ownership of the review process in relation to identifying those people they wish to attend their annual statement review meeting, i.e. parents/carers, as well as particular school staff and multi-agency professionals. Depending on the maturity and age of the pupil, they may also take responsibility for deciding upon the agenda for their review meeting, and what examples of their achievements they wish to present as examples of progress, not only in relation to their area of special educational need, but also in relation to the five Every Child Matters well-being outcomes. Figure 5.1 provides a model template to support an SEN pupil in planning for their annual statement review meeting.

This review meeting belongs to: _____ **I wish to invite to the meeting:** • _____ • _____ • _____ • _____ • _____ • _____ **I want the meeting to be held at:** _____ On the _____	**What has worked best for me:** **What hasn't gone so well for me:**
What I want to talk about at the meeting is: • • • • •	**What difference the extra help has made:** **What I want to happen next:**

Figure 5.1 SEN pupil-centered review meeting template

Table 5.1 Examples of work undertaken by external multi-agency professionals working with SEN pupils in schools

Education Welfare Officer	Social Care Worker	School Nurse	Educational Psychologist
• Supports schools in improving pupils' attendance	• Is engaged in rapid response case work	• Provides confidential advice and guidance on a range of health-related issues, including nutrition, exercise, smoking, mental health, drug abuse, sexual health	• Is involved in the early identification of problems and early intervention
• Undertakes targeted individual and group case work	• Supports the CAF process		• Engages in action research to promote increased teacher knowledge of good inclusive practice and raise expectations
• Protects children from the risks of exploitation and harm	• Supports the school's PSHE programme	• Promotes good physical, emotional and mental health, and supports children and young people to make healthy life choices	
• Monitors the licensing of local child employment and child entertainment	• Signposts to specialist services		• Engages in projects to raise pupil achievement and improve provision for BESD pupils
• Is involved in school-based attendance projects	• Provides counselling and mentoring to pupils and their families	• Contributes to the school's PSHE programme and the Healthy Schools initiative	• Supports the professional development of teachers and TAs, and contributes to governor training
• Liaises with Home Education and Out-of-School Learning Services	• Builds relationships between schools and families	• Helps to develop and update the school's health and safety policy and the sex education policy	• Works collaboratively with other multi-agency practitioners
• Provides professional advice and support to schools on safeguarding	• Provides pupil support for bereavement, self-esteem, behaviour and attendance, depression, self-harming, school anxiety/phobia, family violence, substance abuse, bullying, suicidal threats	• Provides advice on healthy eating	• Supports parents/carers as key partners in their child's learning and well-being
• Supports and advises parents to ensure they fulfil their statutory responsibilities with respect to the education of their children		• Contributes to the school's extended services provision by running a drop-in clinic for children, young people and their parents on or near the school site	• Promotes a solution-oriented approach to problem solving in relation to pupil learning, behaviour and well-being
• Is involved in court action – parent prosecutions for their child's school non-attendance.	• Acts as an advocate for children, young people and their families	• Supports individual pupils with long-term medical needs and health plans	• Works with individual children and young people who have severe, complex and challenging needs
	• Helps to identify school staff and other agency practitioners who can help to maximise pupil success.	• Provides immunisation to pupils, where appropriate	• Is involved in the statutory assessment of children with the most complex needs.
		• Runs parent groups.	

(Continued)

Table 5.1 (Continued)

Play Therapist	Speech and Language Therapist	Connexions Personal Adviser	LA SEN Outreach Teacher
• Helps children through the medium of play to understand the issues that are preventing them from living a happy life	• Assesses children's communication needs	• Provides one-to-one support, advice and guidance to pupils aged 13 to 19 on careers, training and employment opportunities	• Provides advice and support on assessing pupils' needs
• Offers children coping strategies to enable them to manage their feelings such as anger, fear, anxiety, depression, conflict	• Provides direct specialist speech therapy sessions to individual and small groups of children	• Acts as an advocate and mediator for young people, particularly those with SEN or those who are vulnerable	• Provides direct teaching to individual and small groups of SEN pupils following specific programmes
• Helps children to relax and enjoy the play experience	• Provides training to teachers and support assistants in delivering speech and language programmes	• Works in partnership with other agencies such as FE Colleges, Youth Service, Social Services, Health Services, Housing, employers and training providers, the voluntary sector	• Undertakes observations on SEN pupils and feedback to teachers and TAs
• Builds up a relationship of trust with the child to enable them to talk about their feelings with ease	• Contributes to whole-school in-service training on speech, language and communication difficulties		• Advises on appropriate SEN resources for learning
• Undertakes an assessment and observation of the child at school and home to identify their needs	• Advises on resources, ICT and communication aids	• Helps young people to access volunteering, community activities or sport	• Gives demonstration lessons
• Works in partnership with parents and carers and other practitioners to advise them on how best to support and meet the child's needs through play, and to build up the child's resilience.	• Helps teachers and TAs to differentiate the curriculum	• Works with parents and carers to enable them to support their child's career aspirations	• Advises on personalised learning approaches and curriculum modifications
	• Liaises with parents/carers on how they can help to support and promote their child's speech, language and communication needs at home	• Accesses community support from the arts, study support and other guidance networks in the local area, particularly in finding work experience placements.	• Contributes to whole-school staff in-service training
	• Monitors and evaluates the impact of speech and language programmes delivered to pupils		• Advises the teachers/SENCOs on specific interventions and programmes for pupils with SEN
	• Works collaboratively with other professionals such as the Educational Psychologist, School Nurse, Occupational Therapist.		• Provides feedback on the progress of SEN/LDD pupils in their specific intervention programmes
			• Liaises with other practitioners and colleagues
			• Liaises with the parents of SEN/LDD pupils and keeps them informed of progress in intervention programmes.

Table 5.1 (Continued)

Specialist Outreach Teacher for Sensory Impairment (HI/VI)	Primary Mental Health Worker (CAMHS)	Occupational Therapist	Physiotherapist
• Undertakes any specialist teaching • Provides practical advice on how to minimise the barriers to learning and enhance curriculum access • Advises on the provision of any specialist equipment, resources or aids to support hearing and vision • Models good practice in meeting the needs of children and young people with sensory impairments • Advises on any special access arrangements for statutory tests and external examinations • Contributes advice to a child or young person's SEN statutory assessment • Provides INSET and bespoke training to staff in schools and Children's Centres on how to remove barriers to learning and participation • Offers advice to parents/carers on home adaptations, and signposts them to further information.	• Undertakes an assessment to identify the child or young person's mental health problems • Promotes positive emotional health and well-being by providing 'drop-in' sessions, workshops, advice and information to parents, school and Children's Centre staff, children and young people on building resilience • Advises on referral and facilitates access to specialist Child and Adolescent Mental Health Service (CAMHS) as appropriate • Liaises and collaborates with other multi-agency professionals, teachers and support staff • Offers direct inputs and short-term interventions with individual and small groups of children • Provides INSET and bespoke training • Supports the implementation of Family SEAL, TaMHS, Healthy Schools and Healthy FE framework.	• Undertakes an assessment and observation of the child/young person to identify the level of difficulties and needs • Provides direct interventions to children and young people who experience difficulties with their practical and social daily living skills • Identifies and puts in place appropriate strategies to remove barriers to learning and participation • Provides advice and training for parents/carers, children's workforce on how best to work with and support a child or young person • Provides programmes of work and interventions delivered by themselves or through others • Offers advice on the type of specialist equipment to use and the modifications to make to the classroom or at home.	• Undertakes an assessment of the child or young person's movement difficulties • Provides direct therapy, physical interventions, advice and support to minimise the barriers to learning and participation • Works in partnership and liaises with other children's workforce practitioners to meet the needs of a child or young person • Provides training and advice to parents/carers, children's workforce practitioners on how best to meet a child's or young person's needs • Provides programmes of work and practical strategies to support a child/young person in different environments • Advises on specialist equipment and appliances • Supports special therapeutic swimming and hydrotherapy.

(Continued)

Table 5.1 (Continued)

Behaviour Support Teacher	Community Police Officer	Family Support Worker	Parent Partnership Advisor
• Undertakes assessments to identify pupils' emotional and behavioural difficulties • Provides direct support and interventions to enable pupils to manage their behaviour and feelings • Provides advice, guidance and support to staff in schools on how to manage pupils' behaviour • Assists staff in schools to deliver relevant programmes and interventions • Advises on target setting and behaviour plans for pupils with BESD • Provides advice and guidance to parents/carers on how to support their child's behaviour at home • Liaises with other multi-agency professionals • Signposts to further information, support and services • Delivers INSET, bespoke training and workshops to school staff and parents.	• Supports schools in reducing truancy and exclusions • Helps to reduce victimisation, criminality and anti-social behaviour within schools and the local community • Helps to identify and work with pupils at risk of becoming victims of crime and bullying, or becoming young offenders • Supports school staff in dealing with incidents of crime, victimisation or anti-social behaviour • Promotes the participation of pupils in the life of the school and in the wider community, e.g. volunteering and youth activities, community projects • Provides educational inputs for pupils in the classroom on aspects of citizenship and personal safety as part of PSHE • Works in partnership with other agencies such as the Youth Offending Team (YOT), Youth Justice and Connexions • Builds positive relationships between the police and young people.	• Identifies the needs of vulnerable families under stress • Offers practical help and advice to families experiencing problems • Helps parents to enhance their home management and parenting skills • Delivers parent workshops and parenting programmes on a range of topics • Assists social care workers in assessing a family's needs • Provides direct short-term emergency care in the family home • Attends case conferences, TAC meetings, review meetings and any court case hearings • Liaises and works in partnership with other multi-agency practitioners • Helps parents to access relevant education, training and employment • Signposts parents to other information, guidance, agencies.	• Listens to parents' concerns • Offers home visits • Offers confidential, impartial advice and information on SEN and SEND legislation/Codes of Practice • Supports parents in meetings • Delivers workshops and holds drop-in sessions at the one-stop shop or other local venues on a variety of relevant SEN topics • Provides information about disagreement arrangements and the Special Educational Needs and Disability Tribunal (SENDIST) • Supports parents and carers in communicating their concerns and views on specific SEN issues to the school • Supports the parents and carers of SEN children in putting their views in writing and in understanding any letters, reports or documents they receive from the local authority, multi-agency professionals or school.

Drawing on external services for support and expertise

The role of multi-agency professionals working with SEN pupils

The key role of multi-agency professionals working with pupils with SEN and/or disabilities is to contribute to removing barriers to learning and participation, by providing universal, targeted and specialist services/provision.

The school's provision map for SEN/Inclusion will record the range of public, private, voluntary and community sector services delivering additional inputs to pupils with SEN and/or disabilities in the setting.

Table 5.1 exemplifies the work typically undertaken by different professionals. This table provides an at-a-glance guide for SENCOs to disseminate to teaching and learning support staff in school.

Developing and evaluating multi-agency partnerships

Multi-agency partnership working is defined in terms of practitioners from more than one agency jointly working together and sharing aims, information, tasks and responsibilities in order to intervene early to prevent any difficulties from becoming worse.

Effective, collaborative, multi-agency partnership working should add value to the existing efforts and work of a school.

SENCOs may find the following checklist of guiding principles useful in ensuring that multi-agency partnership working with pupils and their families is effective.

☑ The role and responsibilities of multi-agency practitioners are explicit and understood.

☑ Procedures and protocols for multi-agency referral, assessment, interventions and service provision are clear.

☑ A common professional language is used between multi-agency practitioners and the SENCO which clarifies acronyms and technical terms.

☑ Multi-agency meetings are held at least once every term with the SENCO to monitor and review the ongoing development of partnership working.

☑ Sufficient time is made available for the SENCO to engage in multi-agency joint working activities, e.g. CAF completion, team around the child (TAC) meetings, lead professional role.

☑ The contributions of multi-agency practitioners are valued and acknowledged.

☑ Opportunities are provided for joint inter-professional training to take place between the SENCO and multi-agency practitioners/professionals.

☑ SEN pupil-level attainment and ECM outcomes data are jointly analysed and utilised to inform multi-agency provision.

☑ Multi-agency practitioners are informed of the SEN and Inclusion priorities on the school's SEN Development/Improvement Plan, and they are clear about their contributions in meeting the relevant priorities.

☑ Multi-agency practitioners and the SENCO are both clear about gathering robust evidence to demonstrate progress and the impact of additional provision and interventions on SEN pupils' learning and well-being outcomes.

SENCOs should find the resource *Effective Multi-Agency Partnerships* (Cheminais, 2009) a valuable asset.

The One Children's Workforce Framework

The Children's Workforce Development Council (CWDC) launched the One Children's Workforce Framework in October 2009 (CWDC, 2009a). This framework is comprisesd of a rainbow of seven coloured arcs based around the Every Child Matters outcomes, making eight areas for focus, which best describe the main elements or themes of workforce reform. These cover:

• a shared identity, purpose and vision

• common values and language

• behaviours focused on positive outcomes for children and young people

• integrated working practices

• a high-quality, appropriately trained workforce

• complementary roles focused around children and young people

• the capacity to deliver and keep children safe.

The framework is accompanied by an online interactive planning and self-assessment One Children's Workforce Tool which was designed to enable Children's Trusts to measure their progress in developing a reformed workforce. The One Children's Workforce Framework and accompanying tool were enhanced and re-launched in October 2009 following their use by the 152 local authorities in England and 2010 has seen the framework further refined and developed to enable those professionals not working in a Children's Trust, i.e. school leaders and SENCOs, to identify how they can fit in with the vision of an integrated children and young people's workforce. SENCOs should find it useful to view the element/theme on integrated working practices in the CWDC One Children's Workforce online interactive tool and to access the questionnaire. Question 51 asks: *Are integrated working practices helping to deliver better outcomes for children* (in your setting)? I would add, *How do you know?* View the framework and tool at: http://onechildrensworkforce. cwdcouncil.org.uk/

OFSTED inspecting the effectiveness of partnerships in promoting learning and well-being

A SENCO will need to have evidence of the impact and outcomes from the additional provision delivered by external multi-agencies, as part of the regular internal and

Table 5.2 Evaluating the effectiveness of multi-agency partnerships

Aspect of partnership working	RAG rating	Evidence and comments	Action and next steps for development/improvement
1. Accessibility of service			
2. Quality and usefulness of information/publicity materials			
3. Procedures and protocols for referral, assessment and provision			
4. Joined-up integrated working and teamwork			
5. Communication and information sharing			
6. Seeking views and feedback on service provision from service users			
7. Practitioners' skills, knowledge, attitudes and values			
8. Inter-professional training and development			
9. Quality of monitoring and evaluation of service impact			
10. Any other aspect of partnership working (please specify)			

Photocopiable:
Rita Cheminais' Handbook for New SENCOs © Rita Cheminais, 2010 (SAGE)

external accountability requirements. This information will feed into the school's SEF.

A SENCO will find the OFSTED guidance with exemplification, along with the inspection grade descriptors, invaluable in making robust judgements about partnership working within their setting (see OFSTED, 2009: 46–7 for the judgement descriptors).

Table 5.2 offers SENCOs a user-friendly evaluation tool to rate the current position using the red, amber, green (RAG) system of partnership effectiveness. It also enables SENCOs to record evidence of aspects of multi-agency partnership working and to identify the next steps for any aspects of partnership working that require further improvement or development.

SENCOs may be interested in a new Multi-Agency Partnership Award. Further information is available at www.ecm-solutions.org.uk

Other external systems of support

The Children's Trust

Although SENCOs are unlikely to be engaged directly with the local authority Children's Trust, it is useful to gain an understanding about its role and function. The notion of the Children's Trust was first mentioned in the government's green paper *Every Child Matters*, which was published in September 2003. Section 10 of the Children Act 2004 places a duty on local authorities and their statutory partners, which includes schools, academies, PRUs and colleges, to cooperate in making arrangements to improve children's lives and their ECM well-being.

The Children's Trust:

- listens to the views of children, young people and their parents/carers in order to identify the type of services to deliver to meet their needs

- promotes joint working between professionals across different services at strategic and front-line operational levels

- ensures the effective commissioning (the planning and delivery) of services for children and young people based on a robust needs analysis

- overcomes any barriers to sharing and using information across services, e.g. eCAF, ContactPoint

- addresses any gaps existing in provision in order to respond to unmet needs, which may include delivering children's workforce training to help build capacity.

Children's Trusts develop the local strategy for improving children and young people's lives by delivering better services in response to local circumstances – for example, by reducing under-achievement in the early years or improving access to services for disabled children. The Children's Trust also focuses on new ways of working to join up services such as the co-location of services in Children's Centres, and multi-agency 'teams around the child'.

It will be important for SENCOs to be kept up to date with the local Children's Trust developments, particularly in relation to the provision of extended services and multi-agency partnerships which pupils with SEN and/or disabilities are likely to be accessing. Children's Trusts would need to feature on the agenda of local authority SENCO network meetings at least once a year.

Further information about the Children's Trust can be found at: www.dcsf.gov.uk/everychildmatters/aims/about/childrenstrusts/

The Centre for Excellence and Outcomes (C4EO) in Children and Young People's Services was launched in July 2008 to further support Children's Trusts in improving outcomes for children, young people and their families by bringing together the best evidence of what works in order to build their capacity in applying this good practice to their local circumstances.

SENCOs should look to the C4EO (2009) progress maps, particularly those for looked-after children and children with disabilities, which include those with emotional and behavioural difficulties. Each progress map as an interactive web-based tool is linked to best practice research, national, regional and local data, various resources and a series of challenge questions, against which professionals can evaluate provision in their own areas and partnerships.

The following challenge questions/Outcomes Based Accountability (OBA) are based on the C4EO (2009) progress map:

1. What is your vision for improving the participation of disabled children or young people in accessing services in your school/setting?

2. How do you know if disabled children and their parents consider services to be fully accessible in your school/setting?

3. What outcomes do you want for these children or young people?

4. How could you measure these outcomes for disabled children or young people?

5. What is your current progress?

6. Who are the partners you need to help you improve service accessibility for disabled children and young people in your school/setting?

7. What do disabled children think about the services on offer in school?

8. What works really well in improving the outcomes you want for disabled children and young people?

9. What do you propose to do next?

SENCOs can view the progress maps and further materials at www.c4eo.org.uk

The National Service Framework

The National Service Framework (NSF) for Children, Young People and Maternity Services, introduced by the Children Act 2004, consists of a set of 11 evidence-based quality standards for integrated children's health, social care and some education services, which measure performance and progress over an agreed timescale. They enable school leaders, heads of Children's Centres and SENCOs to assess and evaluate collaborative activity from external agencies and feed this evidence into a school's SEF:

- NSF Standards 1 to 5 relate to universal services.

- NSF Standards 6 to 10 cover services for children and young people requiring more specialised care, treatment and support.

- NSF Standard 11 relates to services for pregnant women and their partners.

The NSF standards are supported by exemplar materials which illustrate a child's journey from initial identification, through early childhood to age 16, and beyond school into early adulthood (up to the age of 19). They demonstrate how a child's additional needs can be met by schools and services working together in partnership. Each exemplar cross-references actions to the relevant NSF standard and demonstrates best practice in the successful integration of children's services through the use of the CAF and the team around the child process.

SENCOs will be particularly interested in viewing the NSF standard exemplars that focus on asthma and the Autistic Spectrum Disorders (ASD). SENCOs may find the NSF exemplars valuable in relation to:

- providing a benchmark for judging the quality of a multi-agency involvement at school level

- signposting to further information and resources relating to particular NSF standards

- promoting further ongoing discussions on integrated multi-agency partnership working at local SENCO network meetings and SENCO e-forums, as well as between SENCOs and multi-agency practitioners

- supporting and informing SEN provision mapping

- supporting SENCOs in undertaking small-scale school-based action research related to multi-agency provision

- supporting the SENCO in the delivery of school-based in-house training on SEN, disability and partnerships with external agencies.

The NSF can be accessed and downloaded from the following website: www.dh.gov. uk/en/Healthcare/Children/NationalServiceFrameworkdocuments/index.htm

ContactPoint

ContactPoint is part of the government's Every Child Matters change for children programme. It is an electronic computer-based directory which is designed to make it easier and quicker for authorised professionals in the children's workforce to identify who else is working with the same child or young person.

ContactPoint improves the exchange of information between different agencies. The Children Act 2004 and the Children Act 2004 Information Databases (England) Regulations 2007 provide the legal basis for ContactPoint.

The Department for Children, Schools and Families (DCSF) and local authorities are responsible for ContactPoint. ContactPoint users in children's services and public organisations such as the police, schools and Children's Centres have to be authorised by a local authority. ContactPoint became fully operational in May 2009.

ContactPoint holds only the basic identifying information for each child or young person up to the age of 18 in England, which includes:

- the name, address, gender, date of birth and unique identifying number for each child

- the name and contact details for:

  - parents or carers

  - the educational setting

  - the primary medical practitioner, e.g. GP practice

  - other practitioners working with the child, e.g. a health visitor, social worker, lead professional

  - any indication of the existence of a CAF.

Information is automatically updated but ContactPoint does not contain any case sensitive information such as case notes, assessments, medical data or examination results.

Once a young person reaches the age of 18, their information is removed from the ContactPoint database and retained for six years in a safe archive until it is subsequently destroyed after that period of time. The records of some young people, however, i.e. those who have learning difficulties which make them more vulnerable in adulthood, will stay on ContactPoint until they are 25. Parents can ask the local authority ContactPoint Manager for access to the information about their child in ContactPoint. The local authority is under no obligation to disclose ContactPoint information to a parent for safeguarding reasons. If the child is aged 12 or over, the right to access the information belongs to him or her.

SENCOs are likely to be identified as one of the authorised professionals able to use and access ContactPoint. As users of the system, their enhanced CRB certificate will need to be renewed every three years. The ContactPoint system is password-protected to ensure security to access. SENCOs should ensure they obtain training in the use of ContactPoint from the local authority. Further information about ContactPoint can be found on the following website: www.dcsf.gov.uk/everychildmatters/strategy/deliveringservices/contactpoint/

The Common Assessment Framework process

The Common Assessment Framework (CAF), as part of the government's Every Child Matters change for children programme, is designed to support earlier intervention, improve integrated multi-agency working and reduce bureaucracy by providing one joint holistic common assessment, thereby reducing the number of separate referrals and assessments for a child or young person with additional needs.

A common assessment is completed only when:

- there is agreement that the child or young person is not making the expected progress in the Every Child Matters well-being outcomes

- the child or young person requires the support of more than one professional or agency, i.e. beyond universal service provision, moving on to targeted and specialist provision to enable them to achieve their full potential.

A SENCO needs to remember that not all children and young people with SEN will require a common assessment. Children with SEN who are progressing well, or whose needs are already being successfully met, do not need to go through the common assessment process. In addition, where a child with SEN and/or disabilities is believed to be at risk of, or has experienced significant harm, child protection and safeguarding procedures are followed immediately, as this critical situation goes far beyond the CAF process.

How the Common Assessment Framework is used

The common assessment framework (CAF) is:

- used nationally for children and young people with additional needs who are vulnerable, who have acute needs, or who are a complex case, all requiring more than one agency's involvement

- used by all those multi-agency practitioners/professionals working with the child or young person to record an assessment and the agreed outcomes

- used to support a referral to another agency or other services

- built upon where a further specialist assessment is required.

Before a CAF is started, the parents, child or young person must be consulted to obtain their agreement to proceed with the CAF process. A parent may agree to complete a CAF, but refuse to give their consent for information to be shared with other agencies. Children over the age of 18, or aged between 12 and 16, who are judged to be 'competent', can give their consent in instances where parents refuse to be engaged in the CAF process or refuse information to be shared across agencies. A parent cannot override the child or young person's consent in such instances. A SENCO should not push to get parental consent to share information, especially if it would compromise the child or young person's safety by putting them at risk of harm or abuse from their parents. A CAF can still be undertaken even when a family may refuse to share information, and it is in the best interests of the child or young person to do so. The child, young person and family should be informed that the CAF is being undertaken in order to secure the necessary services to meet that child's or young person's needs.

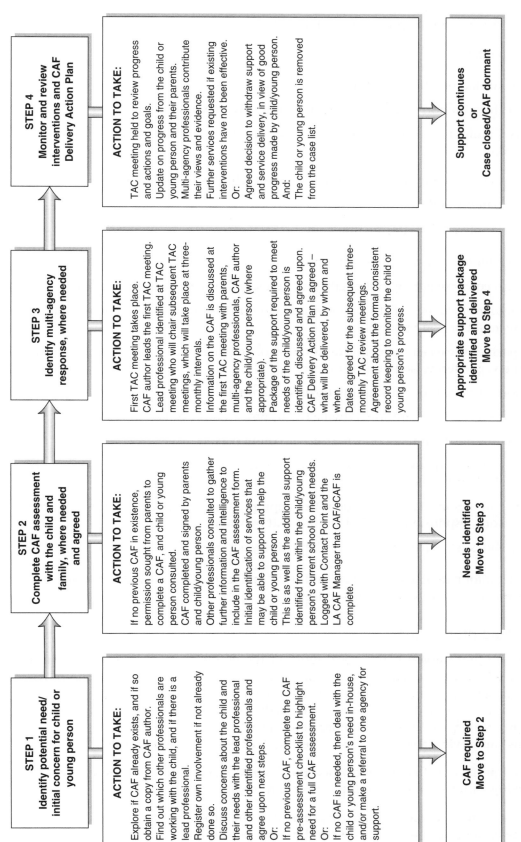

STEP 1
Identify potential need/ initial concern for child or young person

ACTION TO TAKE:

Explore if CAF already exists, and if so obtain a copy from CAF author.
Find out which other professionals are working with the child, and if there is a lead professional.
Register own involvement if not already done so.
Discuss concerns about the child and their needs with the lead professional and other identified professionals and agree upon next steps.
Or:
If no previous CAF, complete the CAF pre-assessment checklist to highlight need for a full CAF assessment.
Or:
If no CAF is needed, then deal with the child or young person's need in-house, and/or make a referral to one agency for support.

CAF required
Move to Step 2

STEP 2
Complete CAF assessment with the child and family, where needed and agreed

ACTION TO TAKE:

If no previous CAF in existence, permission sought from parents to complete a CAF, and child or young person consulted.
CAF completed and signed by parents and child/young person.
Other professionals consulted to gather further information and intelligence to include in the CAF assessment form.
Initial identification of services that may be able to support and help the child or young person.
This is as well as the additional support identified from within the child/young person's current school to meet needs.
Logged with Contact Point and the LA CAF Manager that CAF/eCAF is complete.

Needs identified
Move to Step 3

STEP 3
Identify multi-agency response, where needed

ACTION TO TAKE:

First TAC meeting takes place.
CAF author leads the first TAC meeting. Lead professional identified at TAC meeting who will chair subsequent TAC meetings, which will take place at three-monthly intervals.
Information on the CAF is discussed at the first TAC meeting with parents, multi-agency professionals, CAF author and the child/young person (where appropriate).
Package of the support required to meet needs of the child/young person is identified, discussed and agreed upon.
CAF Delivery Action Plan is agreed – what will be delivered, by whom and when.
Dates agreed for the subsequent three-monthly TAC review meetings.
Agreement about the formal consistent record keeping to monitor the child or young person's progress.

Appropriate support package identified and delivered
Move to Step 4

STEP 4
Monitor and review interventions and CAF Delivery Action Plan

ACTION TO TAKE:

TAC meeting held to review progress and actions and goals.
Update on progress from the child or young person and their parents.
Multi-agency professionals contribute their views and evidence.
Further services requested if existing interventions have not been effective.
Or:
Agreed decision to withdraw support and service delivery, in view of good progress made by child/young person.
And:
The child or young person is removed from the case list.

Support continues
or
Case closed/CAF dormant

Figure 5.2 At-a-glance guide to the CAF process

Photocopiable:
Rita Cheminais' Handbook for New SENCOs © Rita Cheminais, 2010 (SAGE)

Figure 5.2 provides a step-by-step guide to the CAF process for a SENCO.

A good quality CAF form:

- avoids jargon and acronyms
- has information which is clearly and concisely presented
- uses bullet points to list information for the three domains on the form which cover:
  - development of an unborn baby, infant, child or young person
  - parents and carers
  - family and environmental issues
- has information which is fit for purpose, well-ordered and non-judgemental
- gives equal weighting to strengths and needs, with strengths being mentioned first
- provides evidence of the involvement, comments and views of parents and of the child or young person
- specifies the exact frequency or duration of an issue and need, rather than using the vague terms 'sometimes' or 'often'
- doesn't have too many empty boxes or gaps left
- presents evidence informed by fact with observations linked to analysis
- focuses on the impact on the child or young person
- identifies conclusions, solutions and actions which are clear, appropriately pitched and achievable
- has an action plan which identifies appropriate priorities and actions and the persons responsible for what actions and by when
- provides realistic timescales for the delivery action plan.

Further information about the CAF and eCAF can be found at: www.dcsf.gov.uk/every childmatters/strategy/deliveringservices1/caf/

The lead professional

The lead professional is the practitioner in the children's workforce who is most involved with the child/young person. Their key role is to coordinate the provision of services from more than one agency or organisation, based on the child's or young person's identified additional needs. The lead professional pulls together the inputs required from a number of agencies to create an integrated package of joined-up services that can address the child's or young person's needs.

A lead professional is required when there are three or more agencies involved in working with the child or young person and their family.

The lead professional is usually nominated at the first multi-agency meeting with the team around the child. The child, young person and their parents should be consulted about who they would prefer to be the lead professional. The lead professional may change over time as the needs of the child or young person alter.

The SENCO may be identified as the lead professional by a child, young person or their parents. Where this is the case, the demands of the role with its additional responsibilities should be taken into account and reflected in the SENCO's job description. The SENCO as lead professional will need access to administrative support. They must also have accessed local training to prepare them for the role, and ideally have networked with another SENCO who has already experienced being a lead professional in the CAF process.

The key role of the lead professional

The key role of the SENCO as lead professional is to:

- act as a single point of contact and as an advocate for the child, young person and their family

- be a 'gatekeeper' for information sharing

- ensure the child or young person and their parents are kept informed about and fully understand the purpose and outcomes of the multi-professional team around the child (TAC) meetings they attend

- promote and coordinate integrated working between agencies to meet the needs of the child or young person

- foster good communication between the family and all the agencies involved

- coordinate and chair the review process, holding multi-agency TAC meetings every three months

- be proactive in engaging the appropriate services and resources to meet the needs of the child or young person

- pull together the overall evidence from the ongoing monitoring and evaluation of service interventions to feed into the CAF review

- maintain the records of all planning meetings, TAC meetings and related lead professional activity

- ensure any professionals unable to attend TAC meetings provide updates on their work with the child or young person, to feed into the meeting and into the follow-up CAF review paperwork

- inform the local authority CAF Manager of any change in the lead professional, particularly where the SENCO is unable to continue the role due to competing priorities.

Further information about the lead professional can be accessed at:
www.dcsf.gov.uk/everychildmatters/strategy/managersandleaders/leadprofessional/

The team around the child (TAC)

The government first made reference to the team around the child (TAC) in its green paper *Every Child Matters* (DfES, 2003d). The TAC was recommended by the government in the Children Act 2004 as being an effective model of multi-agency collaborative partnership working in which a range of different practitioners and professionals could come together to help, support and meet the needs of an individual child or young person with additional, acute or more complex needs.

The TAC is a needs-led, evolving, small team of professionals who work together to deliver coordinated, joined-up services and interventions in order to address the root cause of a child or young person's difficulties.

A SENCO may be engaged in TAC meetings, either when they are identified as the lead professional, and therefore are responsible for coordinating meetings, or when a pupil with SEN and/or disabilities is subject to a CAF.

Further information about the TAC can be found in the publication entitled *The Team Around the Child (TAC) and the Lead Professional* (CWDC, 2009b).

Points to remember

- Parents are equal partners in having a say about their child's SEN provision.
- The role of multi-agency professionals is understood by key stakeholders.
- Parents requesting information from ContactPoint about their child must be directed to the local authority ContactPoint Manager.
- When a SENCO initiates and completes a CAF, they will be responsible for convening the very first team around the child meeting.
- The role of the lead professional should be included in the SENCO's job description.

Further activities

The following questions, focused on aspects covered in this chapter, meet the requirements of the National Award for Special Educational Needs Coordination, and support reflection and professional development:

1. How could you further improve the involvement of parents and carers in decision making relating to SEN provision?

2. How would you ensure the views of SEN pupils, and particularly those with communication difficulties, are obtained?

3. Focusing on one aspect of multi-agency partnership working in your school or education setting that requires further development, identify the strategies you would adopt to address this issue.

4. Devise a parent-friendly leaflet that would explain in simple terms the common assessment framework, the team around the child, and the role of the lead professional.

5. Write an evaluative paragraph to include in the school's SEF, Section A4.5, on the effectiveness of partnerships in promoting SEN pupils' learning and well-being.

Downloadable materials

For downloadable materials for this chapter visit www.sagepub.co.uk/ritacheminais

Figure 5.1 SEN pupil-centered review meeting template

Figure 5.2 At-a-glance guide to the CAF process

Table 5.2 Evaluating the effectiveness of multi-agency partnerships

Acronyms and Abbreviations

ADD — attention deficit disorder

ADHD — attention deficit hyperactivity disorder

AEN — additional educational needs

AHDC — Aiming High for Disabled Children

ALS — additional literacy support

APP — assessing pupil progress

ASD — autistic spectrum disorder

AST — advanced skills teacher

AWPU — age weighted pupil unit

BAS — British Ability Scales

BECTA — British Educational Communications and Technology Agency

BESD — behavioural, emotional and social difficulties

BEST — behaviour education support team

BPVS — British Picture Vocabulary Scale

CAF — common assessment framework

CAFCASS — Children and Family Court Advisory and Support Service

CAMHS — child and adolescent mental health service

CAT — cognitive ability test

CD — compact disc

CEOP — Child Exploitation and Online Protection

C4EO — Centre for Excellence and Outcomes

CFSEI — culture free self-esteem inventory

COP	code of practice
CPD	continuing professional development
CRB	criminal records bureau
CVA	contextual value added
CWDC	Children's Workforce Development Council
CYP	children and young people
DASH	detailed assessment of speed handwriting
DCSF	Department for Children, Schools and Families
DDA	Disability Discrimination Act
DED	Disability Equality Duty
DES	Disability Equality Scheme
DFEE	Department for Education and Employment
DFES	Department for Education and Skills
DH	Department of Health
DME	dual and multiple exceptionalities
DOB	date of birth
DRC	Disability Rights Commission
DVD	digital versatile disc
EAL	English as an additional language
EBD	emotional and behavioural difficulties
ECM	Every Child Matters
ELS	early literacy support
EMA	ethnic minority achievement
EP	educational psychologist
EYFS	early years foundation stage
FE	further education

FFT	Fischer Family Trust
FLS	further literacy support
FMSIS	Financial Management Standards in Schools
FSM	free school meals
FTE	full-time equivalent
GCSE	General Certificate of Secondary Education
GL	Granada Learning
GORT	Gray oral reading tests
GP	General Practitioner
GROW	goal reality options will
GSRT	Gray silent reading tests
GTC	General Teaching Council for England
HI	hearing impaired
HLTA	higher level teaching assistant
HMI	Her Majesty's Inspector
HORT	Hodder oral reading test
ICT	information communication technology
IDP	Inclusion Development Programme
IEP	individual education plan
INCO	inclusion coordinator
IQ	intelligence quotient
IQS	Institutional Quality Standards
ISB	individual school budget
INSET	in-service education and training
ITE	initial teacher education
ITT	initial teacher training

KS	Key Stage
LA	local authority
LAC	looked after child
LDD	learning difficulties and/or disabilities
LEA	local education authority
LMS	local management of schools
LSA	learning support assistant
MAT	matrix analogies test
MFL	modern foreign language
MIS	management information system
MLD	moderate learning difficulties
NASEN	National Association of Special Educational Needs
NC	National Curriculum
NCSL	National College for School Leadership
NGFL	National Grid for Learning
NQT	newly qualified teacher
NSF	National Service Framework
NSPCC	National Society for the Prevention of Cruelty to Children
NVR	non verbal reasoning
OBA	outcomes based accountability
ODD	oppositional defiance disorder
OFSTED	Office for Standards in Education, Children's Services and Skills
PA	prior attainment
PASS	pupil attitude to self and school
PC	personal computer
PCT	Primary Care Trust

PDA	personal digital assistant
PE	physical education
PEP	personal education plan
PRU	pupil referral unit
PSHE	personal, social and health education
QCA	Qualifications and Curriculum Authority
QCDA	Qualifications and Curriculum Development Agency
QFT	quality first teaching
QTS	Qualified Teacher Status
RAG	red, amber, green
RAISE	Reporting and Analysis for Improvement through School Self-Evaluation
RE	religious education
RM	Research Machines
SAT	standard assessment test
SALT	speech and language therapist
SE	socio economic
SEAL	social, emotional aspects of learning
SEF	self-evaluation form
SEN	special educational needs
SENCO	Special Educational Needs Coordinator
SEND	special educational needs and/or disability
SENDIST	Special Educational Needs and Disability Tribunal
SIMS	school information management system
SLC	speech, language and communication
SLCN	speech, language and communication needs
SLD	severe learning difficulties

SLT   senior leadership team

SX   school extended

TA   teaching assistant

TAC   team around the child

TAMHS   targeted mental health in schools

TDA   Training and Development Agency for Schools

TEAM   together each achieves more

TOWRE   test of word reading efficiency

TSO   The Stationery Office

TTA   Teacher Training Agency

TTRB   Teacher Training Resource Bank

UNCRC   United Nations Convention on the Rights of the Child

VAK   visual, auditory and kinaesthetic

VI   visual impairment

WIAT   Wechsler individual achievement test

WISC   Weschler Intelligence Scale for Children

WRAT   wide range achievement test

YOT   Youth Offending Team

Glossary

Action research   is the investigation into a problem, topic or issue, which, on the basis of the information collected, draws conclusions and makes recommendations to improve practice, or resolve a problem.

Age weighted pupil unit   is the sum of money allocated to a school for each pupil according to age.

Bullying   is any behaviour by an individual or group of pupils which is repeated over time, that intentionally hurts another person or group of pupils either physically or emotionally.

Change   is a developmental process which reassesses existing beliefs, values and assumptions in order to introduce new policies and new ways of working to improve upon current practice.

Children's Trusts   bring together services for children and young people in a local area in order to improve outcomes.

Coaching   is a structured, sustained process that enables the development of a specific aspect of a professional learner's practice, which is solution-focused in its approach.

Common Assessment Framework   is a holistic assessment process used by professionals and front-line practitioners in the children's workforce to assess the additional needs of children and young people at the first signs of difficulty.

ContactPoint   is an electronic computer-based information sharing system that offers children's services professionals a quick means of finding out which other practitioners from external agencies and organisations are working with the same child or young person.

Contextual value added   compares the progress made by each pupil with the average progress made by similar pupils in similar schools.

Delegation   is the process of entrusting somebody else with the appropriate responsibility for the accomplishment of a particular activity.

Disability   describes the condition of any individual who has a physical or mental impairment which has a substantial and long-term adverse effect on their ability to carry out normal day-to-day activities.

Distributed leadership   refers to the sharing out of aspects of leadership across different levels in a workforce, in order to divide tasks and responsibilities up more equitably.

Dual or multiple exceptionalities   are characteristic of those pupils who have a special educational need in addition to a gift or talent. They are highly able in that area of giftedness or talent, but the special educational need hinders the expression of their higher ability.

Evaluation   entails judging the quality, effectiveness, strengths and weaknesses of provision, based on robust evidence collected during review and monitoring processes.

Every Child Matters   is a government initiative and strategy aimed at protecting, nurturing and improving the life chances and well-being outcomes of all children and young people, particularly those who are disadvantaged or vulnerable.

Extended services   are the core offer of activities and provision available beyond the school day, which are designed to meet the needs of children and their families, and the wider community.

Inclusion   is concerned with promoting the belonging, presence, participation and achievement of the full diversity of children and young people.

Information sharing   is the passing on of relevant information to other agencies, organisations and individuals who require it in order to deliver better services to children and young people.

Lead professional   is a designated professional from the health, education or social services, who has day-to-day contact with a child or young person, and coordinates and monitors the service provision, acting as a gatekeeper for information sharing.

Learning difficulties and/or disabilities   are characteristic of pupils who have difficulty in acquiring new skills or who learn at a different rate from their peers. The term is used universally across the education, health and social services.

Mentoring   refers to the process of supporting a professional learner through significant career transitions.

Monitoring   is the systematic checking on progress and the gathering of information to establish the extent to which agreed plans, policies, statutory requirements or intervention programmes are being implemented.

Multi-agency working   is where those professionals from more than one agency or service work together, sharing aims, information, tasks and responsibilities in order to intervene early to prevent a child or young person's difficulties becoming worse.

National Service Framework   offers a set of quality standards for health, social care and some education services, which are aimed at reducing inequalities in service provision in order to improve the lives of children and young people.

Outcomes   are the identifiable (positive and negative) impacts of additional interventions and services on children and young people with additional needs. Outcomes also refers to the five Every Child Matters well-being outcomes of: be healthy, stay safe, enjoy and achieve, make a positive contribution and achieve economic well-being.

P levels   are smaller stepped differentiated performance criteria used for assessing the progress of SEN pupils aged between five and sixteen, who are working below the National Curriculum's level 1.

Pedagogy   is the act of teaching and the rationale that support the actions teachers take. It includes what a teacher needs to know and the range of skills that he/she needs to use in order to make effective teaching decisions.

Personalised learning   is the process of tailoring and matching teaching and learning around the way different pupils learn in order to meet their individual needs, interests and aptitudes, enabling them to reach their full potential.

Progress   refers to pupils making at least two levels of progress across a key stage, in relation to their age and prior attainment (starting point).

Provision map   is a strategic management tool which provides a summary and overview of the range of additional and different provision made available to pupils with additional needs, including those with SEN and/or disabilities.

Quality first teaching   refers to the daily repertoire of teaching strategies and techniques used for all pupils in the mainstream classroom that ensures pupils' progression in learning.

RAISEonline   is a web-based system which contains data about a school's basic characteristics, attainment and progress in the core subjects, to support evaluation and target setting.

Reading age   comes from a comparison. A pupil's ability to read at a given age is tested and compared with the average reading ability of other children of that same age.

Risk assessment   is the careful examination of what could cause harm to an individual or group of people, which enables the person in charge to weigh up whether enough precautions have been taken and if any further action needs to be taken to prevent potential harm occurring.

Self-evaluation   is the ongoing, formative, rigorous, evidence-gathering process, embedded in the daily work of the classroom and school, which gives an honest assessment of their strengths, weaknesses and effectiveness.

Strategic leadership   refers to knowing what you want to achieve, being able to justify the direction and finding the best ways to get there. It entails anticipating change or events, envisioning possibilities and empowering and managing through others to gain a consensus and create a strategic change.

Team around the child   is an individualised, personalised and evolving team of a few different practitioners, who will come together to provide practical support in helping an individual child or young person.

Transfer   refers to a child's move from one school or phase of education to another.

Transition   refers to a child's move from one year group to the next in the same school or another education setting.

Underachievement   refers to the mismatch between a child's current levels of attainment and their potential, which results in them not achieving the national expectation at the end of a Key Stage.

Value added   is a measure that shows the difference a school makes to the educational outcomes of pupils, given their starting points.

Further reading and references

ACE (1997) *Tribunal Toolkit: Going to the Special Educational Needs Tribunal*. London: Advisory Centre for Education.

Audit Commission (2002) *Special Educational Needs: A Mainstream Issue*. Wetherby: Audit Commission.

Audit Commission (2008) *SEN/AEN Value for Money Resource Pack for Schools*. Wetherby: Audit Commission.

Becta (2003) *Managing Special Needs: Recording and Reporting Using ICT*. Coventry: British Educational Communications and Technology Agency.

Becta (2004) *Data Protection and Security: A Summary for Schools*. Coventry: British Educational Communications and Technology Agency.

Belibin, M.R. (1993) *Team Roles at Work*. Oxford: Butterworth-Heinemann.

Belbin, M.R. (2000) *The Evoluation of Human Behaviour and its Bearing on the Future*. Cambridge: Belbin Associates.

Cheminais, R. (2001) *Developing Inclusive School Practice: A Practical Guide*. London: David Fulton.

Cheminais, R. (2003) *Closing the Inclusion Gap: Special and Mainstream Schools Working in Partnership*. London: David Fulton.

Cheminais, R. (2005) *Every Child Matters: A New Role for SENCOs: A Practical Guide*. London: David Fulton.

Cheminais, R. (2007) *Extended Schools and Children's Centres: A Practical Guide*. Abingdon: Routledge.

Cheminais, R. (2009) *Effective Multi-Agency Partnerships: Putting Every Child Matters into Practice*. London: SAGE.

Cheminais, R. (2010) *Special Educational Needs for Newly Qualified Teachers and Teaching Assistants: A Practical Guide*, 2nd edn. Abingdon: Routledge.

C4EO (2009) *Improving the Wellbeing of Disabled Children and Young People Through Improving Access to Positive and Inclusive Activities*. London: The Centre for Excellence and Outcomes in Children and Young People's Services.

Cowne, E. (2008) *The SENCO Handbook: Working within a Whole-School Approach*, 5th edn. Abingdon: Routledge.

CWDC (2009a) *The One Children's Workforce Framework – One Children's Workforce Tool*. Available at: http://onechildrensworkforce.cwdcouncil.org.uk accessed 11 October 2009.

CWDC (2009b) *The Team Around the Child (TAC) and the Lead Professional: A Guide for Practitioners*. Leeds: Children's Workforce Development Council.

Daniels, H. and Porter, J. (2007) *Learning Needs and Difficulties Among Children of Primary School Age: Definition, Identification, Provision and Issues*. Primary Review Research Briefing 5/2. Cambridge: University of Cambridge.

DCSF (2008a) *What is a Children's Trust?* Annesley: Department for Children, Schools and Families.

DCSF (2008b) *Personalised Learning: A Practical Guide*. Annesley: Department for Children, Schools and Families.

DCSF (2008c) *The Education of Children and Young People with Behavioural, Emotional and Social Difficulties as a Special Educational Need*. Annesley: Department for Children, Schools and Families.

DCSF (2008d) *The Inclusion Development Programme*. Annesley: Department for Children, Schools and Families.

DCSF (2008e) *Bullying Involving Children with Special Educational Needs and Disabilities. Safe to Learn: Embedding Anti-bullying Work in Schools.* Annesley: Department for Children, Schools and Families.

DCSF (2008f) *Gifted and Talented Education: Helping to Find and Support Children with Dual or Multiple Exceptionalities.* Annesley: Department for Children, Schools and Families.

DCSF (2008g) *Information Sharing: Pocket Guide.* Annesley: Department for Children, Schools and Families.

DCSF (2009a) *Learning Behaviour: Lessons Learned. A Review of Behaviour Standards and Practices in our Schools.* (Sir Alan Steer). Annesley: Department for Children, Schools and Families.

DCSF (2009b) *Special Educational Needs (SEN): A Guide for Parents and Carers. Revised 2009.* Annesley: Department for Children, Schools and Families.

DCSF (2009c) *Early Identification, Assessment of Needs and Intervention – the Common Assessment Framework for Children and Young People: A Guide for Practitioners.* Annesley: Department for Children, Schools and Families.

DCSF (2009d) *ContactPoint – Lessons Learned from the Early Adopter Phase.* Annesley: Department for Children, Schools and Families.

DCSF (2009e) *Integrated Working Toolkit.* Annesley: Department for Children, Schools and Families.

DCSF (2009f) *Progression Guidance 2009–2010: Improving Data to Raise Attainment and Maximise the Progress of Learners with Special Educational Needs, Learning Difficulties and Disabilities.* Annesley: Department for Children, Schools and Families.

DCSF (2009g) *Identifying and Teaching Children and Young People with Dyslexia and Literacy Difficulties* (Rose Report). Annesley: Department for Children, Schools and Families.

DCSF (2009h) *Children's Trusts: Improving Support for Schools. Improving the Well-being of Children and Young People Through More Effective Children's Services.* Annesley: Department for Children, Schools and Families.

DCSF (2009i) *Children with Special Educational Needs 2009: An Analysis.* Annesley: Department for Children, Schools and Families.

DCSF (2009j) *The Lamb Inquiry: Special Educational Needs and Parental Confidence.* Annesley: Department for Children, Schools and Families.

DfEE (1997) *The SENCO Guide.* London: The Stationery Office.

DfES (2001a) *Inclusive Schooling: Children with Special Educational Needs.* Annesley: Department for Education and Skills.

DfES (2001b) *Special Educational Needs Code of Practice.* Annesley: Department for Education and Skills.

DfES (2001c) *SEN Toolkit.* Annesley: Department for Education and Skills.

DfES (2001d) *Special Educational Needs and Disability Act.* London: The Stationery Office.

DfES (2002) *Accessible Schools: Summary Guidance.* London: Department for Education and Skills.

DfES (2003a) *Targeting Support: Choosing and Implementing Interventions for Children with Significant Literacy Difficulties. Management Guidance.* Annesley: Department for Education and Skills.

DfES (2003b) *Making a Difference: A Guide for Special Educational Needs (SEN) Governors.* Annesley: Department for Education and Skills.

DfES (2003c) *The Report of the Special Schools Working Group.* Annesley: Department for Education and Skills.

DfES (2003d) *Every Child Matters.* London: The Stationery Office.

DfES (2003e) *Success for All: An Inclusive Approach to PE and School Sport* (CD). Annesley Department for Education and Skills.

DfES (2004a) *Every Child Matters: Next Steps.* Annesley: Department for Education and Skills.

DfES (2004b) *Every Child Matters: Change for Children in Schools.* Annesley: Department for Education and Skills.

DfES (2004c) *Teaching Strategies and Approaches for Pupils with Special Educational Needs: A Scoping Study*. RR516. Nottingham: Department for Education and Skills.

DfES (2004d) *Removing Barriers to Achievement: The Government's Strategy for SEN*. Nottingham: Department for Education and Skills.

DfES (2004e) *The Management of SEN Expenditure*. Annesley: Department for Education and Skills.

DfES (2004f) *Freedom of Information Act 2000: Summary Guidance for Governing Bodies*. Annesley: Department for Education and Skills.

DfES (2004g) *The Children Act 2004*. Norwich: Her Majesty's Stationery Office.

DfES (2004h) *Learning and Teaching for Children with Special Educational Needs*. Norwich: Department for Educational and Skills.

DfES (2005a) *Leading on Inclusion*. Annesley: Department for Education and Skills. Available at: http://nationalstrategies.standards.dcsf.gov.uk/node/116685

DfES (2005b) *National Framework for Mentoring and Coaching*. Annesley: Department for Education and Skills.

DfES (2005c) *Promoting Inclusion and Tackling Underperformance. Maximising Progress: Ensuring the Attainment of Pupils with SEN. Part 1: Using Data – Target Setting and Target Getting*. Norwich: Department for Education and Skills. Available at http://nationalstrategies.standards.dcsf.gov.uk/node/97233

DfES (2005d) *Promoting Inclusion and Tackling Underperformance. Maximising Progress: Ensuring the Attainment of Pupils with SEN. Part 2: Approaches to Learning and Teaching in the Mainstream Classroom*. Norwich: Department for Education and Skills.

DfES (2005e) *Promoting Inclusion and Tackling Underperformance. Maximising Progress: Ensuring the Attainment of Pupils with SEN. Part 3: Managing the Learning Process for Pupils with SEN*. Norwich: Department for Education and Skills.

DfES (2006a) *Promoting Inclusion and Tackling Underperformance. Effective Leadership: Ensuring the Progress of Pupils with SEN and/or Disabilities*. Norwich: Department for Education and Skills.

DfES (2006b) *Leading on Intervention*. Annesley: Department for Education and Skills.

DfES (2006c) *Promoting the Disability Equality Duty*. London: Department for Education and Skills.

DfES (2007a) *Every Parent Matters*. Annesley: Department for Education and Skills.

DfES (2007b) *Gifted and Talented Education. Guidance on Preventing Underachievement: A Focus on Dual or Multiple Exceptionality (DME)*. Annesley: Department for Education and Skills.

DfES (2007c) *Implementing the Disability Discrimination Act in Schools and Early Years Settings: A Training Resource for Schools and Local Authorities (A shortened pack)*. London: The Stationery Office.

DH/DfES (2004) *National Service Framework for Children, Young People and Maternity Services*. London: Department of Health/Department for Education and Skills.

DH/DfES (2005) *Managing Medicines in Schools and Early Years Settings*. London: Department of Health/Department for Education and Skills.

DRC (1995) *The Disability Discrimination Act*. London: Her Majesty's Stationery Office.

DRC (2002) *Code of Practice for Schools: Disability Discrimination Act 1995, Part 4*. London: The Stationery Office/Disability Rights Commission.

DRC (2005) *The Disability Discrimination Act*. London: Disability Rights Commission.

Dyson, A., Farrell, P., Hutcheson, G., Polat, F. and Gallannaugh, F. (2004) *Inclusion and Pupil Achievement*. Nottingham: Department for Education and Skills.

East, V. and Evans, L. (2006) *At a Glance: A Practical Guide to Children's Special Needs*, 2nd edn. London: Continuum.

Evans, L. (2007) *SENCO at a Glance: A Toolkit for Success*. London: Continuum.

Fullan, M. (1999) *Change Forces: The Sequel*. London: Falmer Press.

Gibson, S. and Blandford, S. (2005) *Managing Special Educational Needs: A Practical Guide for Primary and Secondary Schools*. London: Paul Chapman Publishing.

GTC (2008) *Making SENse of CPD*. London: General Teaching Council for England. Available at www.gtce.org.uk/networks/sen/

HM Treasury/DfES (2007) *Aiming High for Disabled Children (AHDC): Better Support for Families.* Norwich: Her Majesty's Treasury and the Department for Education and Skills.

HMSO (2008) *The Education (Special Educational Needs Co-ordinators) (England) Regulations 2008.* London: The Stationery Office.

House of Commons Education and Skills Committee (2006) *Special Educational Needs: Third Report of Session 2005–2006*, Volumes 1–3. London: House of Commons.

HSE (2006a) *Health and Safety Matters for Special Educational Needs: Legal Issues Including Risk Assessment.* Sudbury: Health and Safety Executive.

HSE (2006b) *Five Steps to Risk Assessment.* Sudbury: Health and Safety Executive.

ICO (2007) *Data Protection Good Practice Note: Taking Photographs in Schools.* London: Information Commissioners Office.

IDEA (2008) *Underachieving School-age Children: Overview Published April 2008.* London: Improvement and Development Agency.

Kirby, A. (2006) *Mapping SEN: Routes Through Identification to Intervention.* Abingdon: Routledge.

Koshy, V. (2009) *Action Research for Improving Educational Practice*, 2nd edn. London: SAGE.

Lewin, K. (1943) 'Defining the "field at a given time"', *Psychological Review* 50: 292–310. Republished in *Resolving Social Conflicts and Field Theory in Social Science,* Washington, DC: American Psychological Association, 1997.

Lorenz, S. (1997) *Psychobabble: A Parent's Guide to Psychological Reports.* Worsley: Stephanie Lorenz.

Macintyre, C. (1991) *Let's Find Why: A Practical Guide to Action Research in Schools.* Edinburgh: Moray House Publications.

Macintyre, C. (2000) *The Art of Action Research in the Classroom.* London: David Fulton.

McNiff, J. (2002) *Action Research for Professional Development: Concise Advice for New Researchers.* Available at: www.jeanmcniff.com/Copy%20booklet%20for%20web%20site.doc accessed 6 September 2009.

NASEN (2001) *Policy Document on the Role of the SEN Co-ordinator.* Tamworth: National Association of Special Educational Needs.

NASEN (2009) *Abbreviations for Inclusion.* Tamworth: National Association for Special Educational Needs.

NCSL/TDA (2009) *Engaging Schools in Sustainable Every Child Matters and Extended Services.* Nottingham: National College for School Leadership and the Training and Development Agency for Schools.

OFSTED (2000) *Evaluating Educational Inclusion.* London: Office for Standards in Education.

OFSTED (2004a) *Special Educational Needs and Disability: Towards Inclusive Schools.* London: Office for Standards in Education.

OFSTED (2004b) *Setting Targets for Pupils with Special Educational Needs.* London: Office for Standards in Education.

OFSTED (2005) *Removing Barriers: A 'Can-do' Attitude.* London: Office for Standards in Education.

OFSTED (2006a) *Inclusion: Does it Matter Where Pupils are Taught? Provision and Outcomes in Different Settings for Pupils with Learning Difficulties and Disabilities.* London: Office for Standards in Education.

OFSTED (2006b) *Extended Schools: A Report on Early Developments.* London: Office for Standards in Education.

OFSTED (2008a) *How Well New Teachers are Prepared to Teach Pupils with Learning Difficulties and/ or Disabilities.* London: Office for Standards in Education, Children's Services and Skills.

OFSTED (2008b) *The Impact of Children's Centres and Extended Schools.* London: Office for Standards in Education.

OFSTED (2009) *The Evaluation Schedule for Schools. Guidance and Grade Descriptors for Inspecting Schools in England under Section 5 of the Education Act 2005, from September 2009.* London: Office for Standards in Education, Children's Services and Skills.

QCA (2001) *Supporting School Improvement: Emotional and Behavioural Development.* London: Qualifications and Curriculum Authority.

QCA (2005) *Using the P Scales: Assessing, Moderating and Reporting Pupil Attainment in English, Mathematics and Science at Levels P4 to P8*. Norwich: Qualifications and Curriculum Authority.

QCA (2009) *Planning, Teaching and Assessing the Curriculum for Pupils with Learning Difficulties*. London: Qualifications and Curriculum Authority.

QCDA (2009a) *Key Stage 2 2010: Assessing Pupils' Eligibility for Additional Time*. London: Qualifications and Curriculum Development Agency.

QCDA (2009b) *Key Stage 2 2010: Assessment and Reporting Arrangements*. London: Qualifications and Curriculum Development Agency.

QCDA (2009c) *Key Stage 2 2010: Guidance on Completing Applications for up to 25 Per Cent Additional Time*. London: Qualifications and Curriculum Development Agency.

TDA (2009) *Specification for Nationally Approved Training for Special Educational Needs Coordinators (SENCOs) New to the Role, Leading to the Award of the National Award for SEN Co-ordination*. London: Training and Development Agency for Schools.

The Children's Society (2006) *A Young Person's Guide to Changing Schools: Moving from Primary to Secondary School*. London: The Children's Society.

Thomas, K. and Kilmann, R. (1974) *Conflict Mode Instrument*. Newport Coast, CA: Kilmann Diagnostics.

TSO (2006) *The Government's Response to the Education and Skills Committee report on Special Educational Needs*. Norwich: The Stationery Office.

TSO (2007) *Implementing the Disability Discrimination Act (DDA) in Schools and Early Years Settings*. Norwich: The Stationery Office.

TSO (2008) *The Education (Special Educational Needs Coordinators) (England) Regulations 2008*. London: The Stationery Office.

TTA (1998) *National Standards for Special Educational Needs Coordinators*. London: Teacher Training Agency.

TTA (2001) *Using the National Standards for Special Educational Needs Coordinators*. London: Teacher Training Agency.

Wallace, E., Smith, K., Pye, J., Crouch, J., Ziff, A. and Burston, K. (2009) *Extended School Survey of Schools, Pupils and Parents: A Quantitative Study of Perceptions and Usage of Extended Services in Schools*. Annesley: Ipsos MORI.

Warnock, M. (2005) *Special Educational Needs: A New Look*. Paper 11. London: Philosophy of Education Society of Great Britain.

Index

Note: page numbers in *italic* refer to figures and tables.

Exciting Education Texts from SAGE

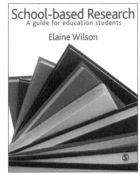

978-1-4129-4850-0

978-1-4129-4818-0

Achieving your PTLLS Award

Mary Francis
Jim Gould

978-1-84787-917-2

Introduction to Research Methods in Education

Keith F Punch

978-1-84787-018-6

A Toolkit for the effective Teaching Assistant

2nd Edition

Maureen Parker, Chris Lee, Stuart Gunn,
Kitty Heardman, Rachael Hincks,
Mary Pittman and Mark Townsend

978-1-84787-943-1

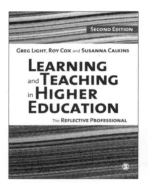

SECOND EDITION

GREG LIGHT, ROY COX and SUSANNA CALKINS

LEARNING and TEACHING in HIGHER EDUCATION

The REFLECTIVE PROFESSIONAL

978-1-84860-008-9

TEACHING SCIENCE

TONY LIVERSIDGE
MATT COCHRANE
BERNARD KERFOOT
JUDITH THOMAS

978-1-84787-362-0

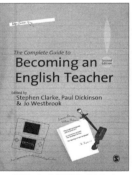

The Complete Guide to
Becoming an English Teacher

Edited by
Stephen Clarke, Paul Dickinson
& Jo Westbrook

978-1-84787-289-0

3rd Edition

Daniel Muijs and David Reynolds
Effective Teaching
Evidence and Practice

978-1-84920-076-9

Find out more about these titles and our wide range of books for education students and practitioners at **www.sagepub.co.uk/education**